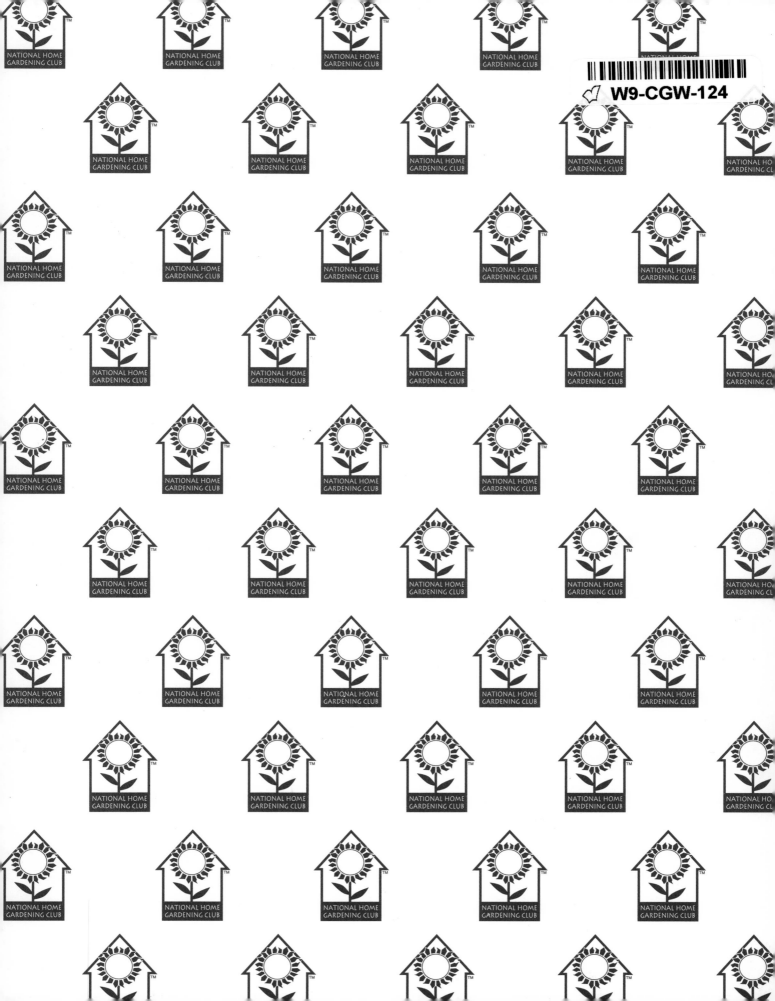

W9-CGW-124

NHGC Member's Cookbook

NHGC
Member's

Cookbook

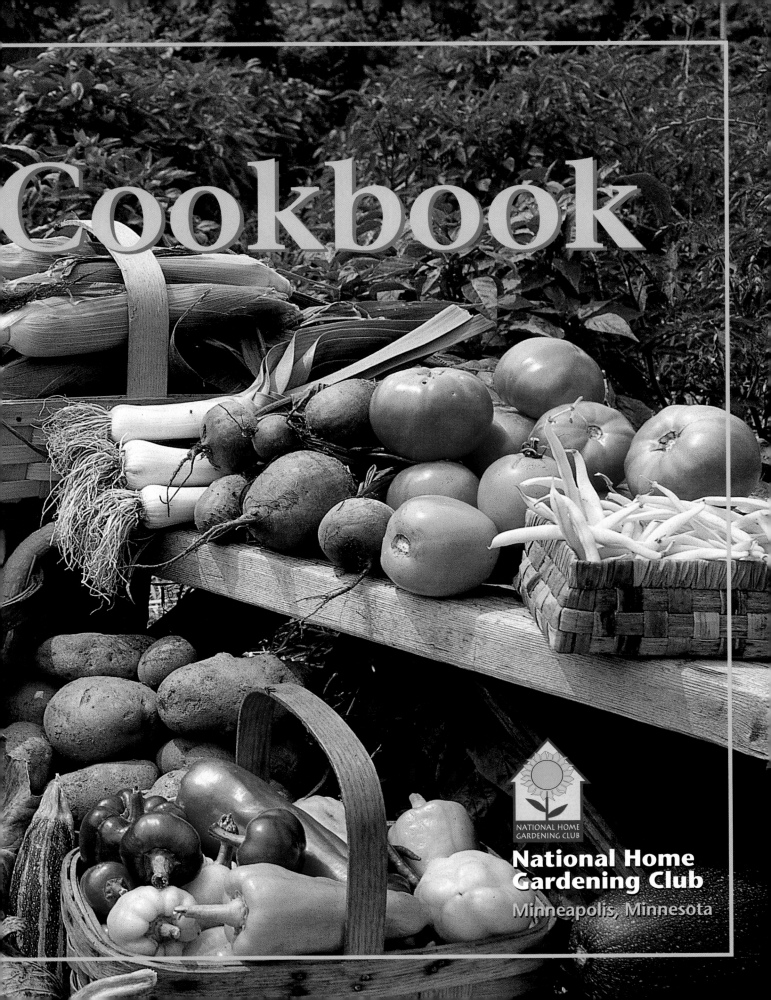

**National Home
Gardening Club**
Minneapolis, Minnesota

NHGC Member's Cookbook

Vice President, Product Marketing/Business Development
Mike Vail

Director of Book and New Media Development
Tom Carpenter

Book Products Development Manager
Steve Perlstein

Book Development Coordinator
Dan Kennedy

Book Development Assistant
Michele Teigen

Photo Editor
Jennifer Block

Editor
Ellen Boeke

Design and Production
Clarinda Color

Illustrations
Bill Reynolds

Photo Credits

Jim Block: 29, 66, 67, 69, 74, 79, 83, 89, 111, 126, 130, 169; Walter Chandoha: i, ii-iii, vi, 9, 11, 18, 31, 36, 41, 44, 46, 48, 50, 54, 56, 57, 60, 65, 73, 77 (2), 82 (2), 84, 86 (2), 90, 91, 92, 95, 96, 97, 99, 104, 105, 106, 112 (2), 113, 114, 123, 125, 126, 131, 135, 138, 140, 142, 146, 147, 154, 156, 159, 162, 164, 165, 166, 170, 172, 183; Jeff Johnson: Cover, v (8), 2, 4, 8, 13, 14, 20, 23, 25, 26, 32, 34, 35, 38, 42, 45, 52, 53, 58, 62, 70, 80, 85, 100, 101, 102, 106, 108, 116, 119, 120, 128, 132, 167, 168, 174

ISBN 0-914-697-96-X

National Home Gardening Club
12301 Whitewater Drive
Minnetonka, Minnesota 55343

Contents

From the Garden to the Table

Few pleasures can compare to the taste of food prepared with fruits and vegetables picked from our own backyards and thrown right into the pot. It's why many of us garden in the first place. That's why we are so excited about the NHGC Member's Cookbook.

We solicited recipes from you, our members, and you responded with hundreds and hundreds of submissions. We picked a representative sample of them, and saved the rest for future editions of our member's cookbooks. The selections range from generations-old family recipes to brand new creations; from elaborate concoctions to easy dishes you can whip together in minutes.

Together with beautiful photography and Bill Reynold's charming watercolor illustrations, the result is an exciting, eclectic, and delicious collection of our members' best dishes. We know—those of us at the National Home Gardening Club were lucky enough to be at the photo shoots and sample the dishes after we were done photographing them!

We know you'll enjoy trying the recipes in this cookbook as much as we enjoyed selecting them for you. Good eating, and good gardening!

CHAPTER 1

Breads

Gayl's Sweet Potato Biscuits

4 cups self-rising flour
1/4 cup vegetable shortening
milk
2 sweet potatoes, peeled,
chunked and cooked
bacon grease

In a large mixing bowl, cut the shortening into the flour. Add enough milk to make a stiff dough. Add the sweet potatoes and mix well.

On a floured surface, knead the dough well. Roll it out to 1/2-inch thickness. Cut the dough with a round biscuit cutter and place biscuits on a greased cookie sheet. Put a small drop of bacon grease on top of each biscuit. Bake at 400° oven until the tops are golden brown.

Gayl Fenton
Bidwell, OH

Sweet Potato Biscuits

Rhubarb-Streusel Bread

Bread ingredients:

2-1/2 cups flour
1-1/2 cups diced rhubarb
1 cup brown sugar
1/2 cup white sugar
1 tsp. salt
1 tsp. baking soda
1 cup buttermilk
2/3 cup vegetable oil
1 egg
1 tsp. vanilla

Topping ingredients:

1/2 cup brown sugar
1 tsp. butter, softened
1 tsp. ground cinnamon

Mix all of the dry bread ingredients together. Add wet bread ingredients and mix well. Pour batter into two greased and floured loaf pans. Combine the topping ingredients and sprinkle on top of the loaves. Bake at 350° for 1 hour, or until toothpick inserted in center comes out clean.

Laura Schultz
Wells, MN

Rhubarb Bread

Blueberry Muffins

1/2 cup unsalted butter
1/4 cup fine sugar
1 large egg, beaten
1-1/2 cups milk
2-1/3 cups cake flour, sifted
2 tsp. baking powder
1/4 tsp. salt
1/2 cup blueberries, washed

Cream the butter and the sugar together. Combine the egg with the milk. Sift the dry ingredients together. Alternately add the egg mixture and the dry mixture to the butter and sugar. Do not overmix. Fold in the blueberries. Pour into muffin pans, greased or with liners, and bake at 350° for 20 minutes, or until golden.

LuAn McGinnis
Hattiesburg, MS

Honey Buns

1/3 cup honey
1/4 cup chopped nuts (optional)
4 T. melted butter or margarine, divided
1 10-oz. can refrigerated flaky biscuit dough
2 T. brown sugar
3/4 tsp. ground cinnamon

Cook, then mash the potatoes well. Dissolve the yeast in warm milk. In a large bowl, combine potatoes, milk mixture, the flour, eggs, oil, butter and salt to taste. Beat vigorously until smooth; let dough rest for 2 hours. Pour the dough into a greased casserole or pizza pan. Add your favorite toppings. Bake in a 425° oven for 20 minutes.

HINT: Shrimp is my favorite topping.

Regina Peavy
Big Sandy, TX

Barbara's Sweet Potato Biscuits

2 cups all-purpose flour
1 tsp. baking powder
1 tsp. salt
1 cup mashed cooked
sweet potatoes
1/4 cup shortening
3 tsp. milk

Mix the flour, baking powder and salt with a fork. Cut in the potatoes and shortening until mixture has a coarse crumb consistency. Stir in the milk until the mixture is just moistened. Roll the dough to 1/2-inch thickness. Cut dough with biscuit cutter and bake at 450° until they are golden brown.

HINT: When the biscuits are done, split them in half, add a slice of butter and 1/2 tsp. sugar.

Barbara Holloway
Lincolnton, GA

Bumblebee Bread

3 10-oz. cans refrigerated
biscuit dough
2 cups brown sugar
3/4 cups butter or margarine
1 T. ground cinnamon

Tear each biscuit into four pieces. Spray a pound cake pan or fluted cake pan well with cooking spray and pile the biscuit pieces in it. Melt the sugar, butter and cinnamon together and pour over the biscuits. Bake at 375° for 45 minutes.

Carlene Collins
Monroe, NC

Orange Rolls

Ingredients for dough:

4 cups all-purpose
  flour, divided
1 cup milk, warmed
3 eggs, beaten
1/2 cup sugar
3 T. butter
1 yeast cake (or 1 pkg.
  active dry yeast)
1 T. salt

Ingredients for orange spread:

2 oranges
3/4 cup sugar
1/2 cup butter, softened

Mix all of the dough ingredients well, adding enough milk so it holds together when shaped. Make the dough balls about the size of walnuts. Cook in a large Dutch oven on the top of the stove, or on a large jelly roll pan in a 350° oven for 20 minutes, until browned.

Combine the sauce ingredients and add to the browned dough balls in Dutch oven. Simmer for 30-45 minutes over medium-low heat. Serve with toothpicks on a hot tray or out of a slow cooker.

Maryann Bump
West Allis, WI

Cheddar Cheese Corn Bread

1 cup yellow cornmeal
1/2 cup unbleached
   all-purpose flour
2 tsp. baking powder
1 tsp. baking soda
   pinch salt
1-1/4 cups buttermilk
2 large eggs, lightly beaten
3 T. unsalted butter, melted
1-1/2 cups fresh corn kernels
   (2 medium ears)
1 cup grated sharp
   cheddar cheese
1/4 cup finely shredded
   fresh basil leaves

Preheat the oven to 400° and generously grease an 8-inch baking pan. In a large bowl, stir together the cornmeal, flour, baking powder, baking soda and salt. Mix in the buttermilk, eggs and melted butter. Stir in the corn kernels, cheese and basil. Scrape the batter into the prepared pan and bake for 35-40 minutes, or until golden. Let it cool slightly before serving.

Makes one 8-inch cornbread.

Susan Severance
Missouri City, TX

Cheddar Cheese Corn Bread

Friendship Harvest Loaf

2-1/2 cups all-purpose
flour, sifted
2 cups sugar
1-1/2 tsp. baking soda
1-1/2 tsp. salt
1 tsp. ground cinnamon
1 tsp. ground nutmeg
1/2 cup shortening
1/2 cup water
1-1/2 cups applesauce
1 egg
1/2 cup chopped walnuts
1/2 cup raisins

Sift the dry ingredients together. Add the shortening and water. Beat for 1 minute with an electric mixer. Add the applesauce and egg; mix for 3 minutes. Stir in the nuts and raisins. Pour into two greased and floured loaf pans. Bake at 350° for 35-40 minutes, or until toothpick inserted in center comes out clean.

Zen Donohoe
Porterville, CA

Leaf Lettuce Bread

2 tsp. baking powder
1/2 tsp. baking soda
1/2 tsp. salt
1/8 tsp. ground ginger
1/8 tsp. mace
1 cup sugar
1/2 cup vegetable oil
2 eggs
1/2 tsp. grated lemon peel
1-1/2 cups all-purpose flour
1 cup lightly packed, finely
chopped leaf lettuce
1/2 cup chopped nuts

In a small bowl, mix together the baking powder, baking soda, salt, ginger and mace. In a medium bowl, beat together the sugar, oil, eggs and lemon peel. Mix the small bowl of dry ingredients into the oil mixture, then add the flour and mix until smooth. Stir in the lettuce and nuts.

Bake at 350° until golden brown on top and a wooden toothpick inserted in the center comes out clean (about 50-55 minutes). Cool bread in pan on a wire rack for about 10 minutes. Turn bread out of pan and continue cooling on a rack. Serve slightly warm or cooled.

Makes 1 loaf.

Suzanne Johnston
Marinette, WI

Whole Wheat Bread

*2 pkgs. (or 4 1/2 tsp.) active
dry yeast
1/2 cup warm water (110°-115°)
pinch sugar
3-1/2 cups whole wheat
flour, medium grind
1-1/2 cups quick-cooking
rolled oats
2 tsp. salt
2-1/2 cups skim milk,
heated (110°-115°)
1/2 cup dark molasses
3 cups all-purpose flour*

Dissolve the yeast in the warm water with a pinch of sugar. It should be foamy in approximately 5 minutes. (If not, throw it out and get fresh yeast.) Mix together the wheat flour, oats and salt in a large bowl. Make a well in the center of the mixture. In a separate bowl, combine the milk, molasses and yeast mixture, then pour into the flour and oat mixture. Blend in as much of the all-purpose flour as is needed to make a soft dough.

Turn the dough out of the bowl and knead it for 10 minutes, adding more flour as needed to prevent sticking. Shape into a ball and put back into a clean bowl that has been coated with cooking spray. Turn the dough to grease the top. Let it rise

in a warm place until it has doubled (about 1 to 1-1/2 hours).

Punch the dough down and divide it into two balls. Shape dough into two loaves and place in greased loaf pans. Let it rise again until doubled (about 1 hour). Slash the tops of the loaves and brush with water. You can sprinkle with oats at this point, if desired.

Bake at 350° for 40 minutes, or until each loaf sounds hollow when tapped. Brush with melted butter, cool completely and store in airtight plastic bags. This bread also freezes well.

Gaelen McNamara
Chattanooga, TN

Corn Bread

2 T. bacon fat
3/4 cup cornmeal
1/4 cup all-purpose flour
2 tsp. baking powder
3/4 tsp. salt
1/2 tsp. sugar
1/4 tsp. baking soda
3/4 cup buttermilk
1 egg

Heat the fat in an ovenproof pan (preferably an iron skillet). While this is melting, mix the dry ingredients together. Pour in the buttermilk and the egg and mix well. Pour batter into heated pan and bake at 425° for 20-25 minutes, or until the top is browned and crispy.

HINT: The trick is to never put the fat in the batter, just in the pan.

Betty Taylor
Dallas, TX

Garden Herb Bread

*1-1/4 cups warm water
(110°-115°)
2 T. butter or margarine, melted
3 cups bread flour
(can substitute 1-1/2 cups
whole wheat flour)
2 T. nonfat dry milk
2 T. sugar
2 tsp. rapid-rise yeast,
or 3 T. active dry yeast
1-1/2 tsp. salt
1-1/2 tsp. chives
1-1/2 tsp. marjoram
1-1/2 tsp. thyme
1 tsp. basil*

Combine the water and butter in a bowl. Mix the remaining ingredients and add to the liquid. Mix thoroughly; let dough rest for 15 minutes. Knead the dough until it is soft and elastic. (This is a soft dough.) Place dough in a greased pan and allow it to double in size. Bake at 375° for 30-45 minutes.

HINT: This bread is great for sandwiches, and it can be sliced thin if it is not allowed to rise too much (not more than double in size).

June E. Howes
Keymar, MD

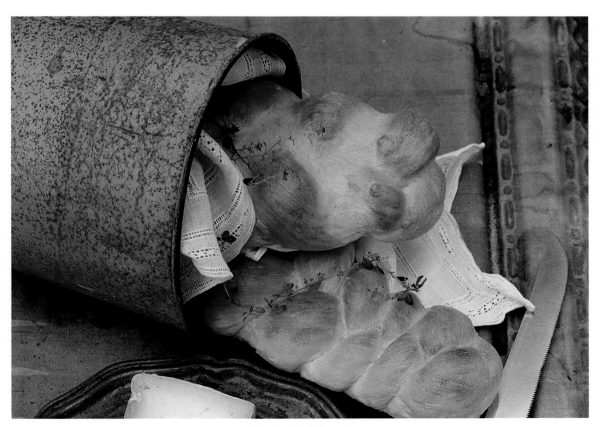

Garden Herb bread.

CHAPTER 2

Appetizers

Boursin (Herbed Cheese Spread)

8 oz. cream cheese, softened
1/4 cup minced fresh herbs (use
at least 4 of the following:
rosemary, thyme, dill, Greek
oregano, marjoram, summer
savory, basil, sage)
1 T. finely chopped fresh parsley
1 T. finely chopped fresh chives
1 T. fresh lemon juice
1 clove garlic, minced
1/2 tsp. Worcestershire sauce
1/2 tsp. dry mustard

Combine all ingredients, mixing
gently and thoroughly. Do not beat.
Cover tightly and refrigerate. When
ready to serve, bring to room
temperature.

Makes 1 cup.

Katherine E. Brock
Piqua, OH

Boursin (Herbed Cheese Spread)

Taco Dip

8 oz. cream cheese
1 cup sour cream
taco seasoning, to taste
shredded lettuce
chopped tomatoes
shredded cheddar cheese
chopped onions (optional)
green or black olives, sliced
salsa
tortilla chips

Cream the cream cheese, sour cream and taco seasoning together. Spread on a tray or large plate. Top with even layers of lettuce, tomatoes, cheese, onions, olives and salsa. Serve with your favorite tortilla chips.

Karel Norton
Waseca, MN

Round Corn Rye Dip

2 round corn rye bread
loaves (unsliced)
1 cup sour cream
1 T. Beau Monde seasoning
1 T. chopped fresh chives
1 T. chopped fresh dill weed
1 T. chopped fresh parsley

Combine all the ingredients (except the bread) and mix well. Cut up one loaf of the corn rye bread into bite-size pieces. Hollow out the center of the other loaf and spoon the dip into it. Serve the cubed bread with filled loaf for dipping.

Debby Gibson
West Hills, CA

PARSLEY

Bacon Cream Cheese Ball

2 8-oz. pkgs. cream
cheese, softened
6-8 strips bacon, cooked
and crumbled
4-5 green onions, chopped
1 tsp. garlic salt

Mix all ingredients together and
chill for 1 hour. Remove from refrigerator 20 minutes before serving.
Serve with your choice of cracker.

Lisa Owens
Tacoma, WA

Cheese Balls

4 oz. American cheese
4 oz. pimento cheese
4 oz. New York cheddar cheese
(or other sharp cheese)
1 medium onion, chopped
1 clove garlic, minced
1-2 hot peppers,
seeded and chopped
1 cup pecans
4 oz. cream cheese
1 tsp. lemon juice
1 T. Worcestershire sauce
chili powder
paprika

Put the American, pimento and
cheddar cheeses, onion, garlic,
peppers and pecans through a fine-
blade food grinder; then mix by
hand. Add the cream cheese, lemon
juice and Worcestershire sauce.
Blend well and form into balls
about the size of a large orange. Roll
balls until well coated in chili
powder and paprika. Chill, slice and
serve.

Lydia Johnson
Freeport, TX

Zucchini Appetizers

3 cups thinly sliced unpeeled
zucchini (about 4 small)
1 cup biscuit mix
4 eggs, beaten
1/2 cup chopped onion
1/2 cup grated fresh
Parmesan cheese
1/2 cup vegetable oil
2 T. chopped fresh parsley
1 clove garlic, minced
1/2 tsp. salt
1/2 tsp. seasoned salt
1/2 tsp. dry oregano leaves
dash pepper

Preheat the oven to 350° and grease a 13 x 9-inch pan. Mix all of the ingredients together and spread in the pan. Bake for 30 minutes, or until golden brown. Cut into 1 x 2-inch squares.

Makes 4 dozen appetizers.

Patricia A. Forrest
Cranberry Lake, NY

Swedish Meatballs

Meatball ingredients:

1-1/2 to 2 lbs. ground beef
1/2-3/4 cup milk
1 small onion, finely chopped
1 egg
1 T. instant coffee
fresh bread crumbs
(from about 4 slices of bread)
1/2 tsp. ground nutmeg
1/2 tsp. garlic powder salt and
pepper to taste

Sauce:

2 cups milk
1 cup cream of mushroom soup
1 cup cream of chicken soup
1 T. chopped fresh parsley
1 T. chopped fresh dill

Mix all of the meatball ingredients well, adding enough milk so it holds together when shaped. Make the meatballs about the size of walnuts. Cook in a large Dutch oven on the top of the stove, or on a large jelly roll pan in a 350° oven for 20 minutes, until browned.

Combine the sauce ingredients and add to the browned meatballs in Dutch oven. Simmer for 30-45 minutes over medium-low heat. Serve with toothpicks on a hot tray or out of a slow cooker.

Maryann Bump
West Allis, WI

Hummus

1 can organic garbanzo beans
1/4 cup sesame tahini
juice from 2 lemons
3-4 cloves of garlic, minced

Mix with an electric mixer until smooth. Serve as dip or spread with pita bread.

Alan Coleman
Lewisville, TX

Hummus

Avocado Dip

1/2 white onion
3 T. lemon juice
4 ripe avocados
1/2 cup picante sauce
3 T. salt

Peel and cube the onion. Place the onion and the lemon juice in a food processor until the onion is chopped very small. Cut the avocados lengthwise and remove the pit and scoop out the green stuff (a great job for kids). Add the scooped-out avocado to the food processor and blend until smooth. Add the picante sauce and salt.

(Wash off the pits and then insert 3 toothpicks into each one — close to the center and in a triangle shape. Fill a pint jar with water and suspend the pits halfway into the water. Put the jar in your kitchen window and wait for your avocado tree to grow.)

Donna May
Greensburg, KY

Cream Cheese Dip

1 pkg. cream cheese, softened
1 jar Accent (monsodium glutamate or MSG)
3 green onions, chopped
1 T. dry onion flakes
1 tsp. dried beef, chopped

Mix all ingredients and chill. Set out 1 hour before serving. This is great on crackers or celery.

Shirley Lewis
Lancaster, KY

Party Cheese Balls

2 8-oz. pkgs. low-fat cream
cheese, softened
8 oz. sharp cheddar cheese,
grated
2 T. Worcestershire sauce
1 T. chopped pimentos
1 T. chopped green pepper
1 tsp. finely chopped green onion
1 tsp. lemon juice
dash cayenne pepper
1 cup finely chopped pecans

Mix the cheeses until well blended. Add all of the other ingredients, except the pecans; mix well. Shape into two balls. Roll each ball in the chopped pecans to coat. Wrap in aluminum foil and chill for at least 24 hours.

These cheese balls freeze well for later use.

Neva Carter
Grand Prairie, TX

Comeback Sauce

1 cup mayonnaise
1 medium onion, grated
1/2 cup vegetable oil
1/4 cup chili sauce
1/4 cup ketchup
juice of 1 lemon
1 T. water
3 cloves garlic, minced
1 tsp. mustard
1 tsp. Worcestershire sauce
1 tsp. black pepper
1 tsp. salt
1/2 tsp. paprika
dash Tabasco sauce

Combine all ingredients. Refrigerate for at least 30 minutes, so that each ingredient can get married to the others.

This sauce can be used as a dip or as a salad dressing. It is great to dip broiled shrimp in. It will last 2 weeks in the refrigerator.

Makes 2 cups or maybe a little more.

Anna Sparks
Hattiesburg, MS

Fried Squash Blossoms

1/2 cup all-purpose flour
1/2 tsp. baking powder
1/4 tsp. garlic salt
1/4 tsp. ground cumin
1 egg
1/2 cup milk
1 T. vegetable oil
oil for frying
12 freshly picked squash
blossoms, washed

In a medium bowl, mix the flour, baking powder, garlic salt and cumin. In a separate bowl, beat the egg, milk and oil together, then add to the dry ingredients. Stir butter well.

In a deep skillet, heat 2 inches of oil to 375˚. Dip the blossoms in the batter and then fry a few at a time until crisp. Drain on paper towels. Serve warm.

Joan Jackson
Lowell, AR

Fried Squash Blossoms

Toasted Almond Party Spread

1 8-oz. pkg. cream cheese,
softened
1-1/2 cups shredded natural
Swiss cheese
1/3 cup salad dressing
2 T. chopped green onions
1/8 tsp. ground nutmeg
1/8 tsp. pepper
1/3 cup, plus additional for
garnish, sliced almonds, toasted

Preheat the oven to 350˚. Combine all of the ingredients, mixing well. Spread the mixture into a 9-inch pie plate. Bake for 15 minutes, stirring half way through. Garnish with additional toasted almonds and serve with party breads.

Kathy Cripe
South Bend, IN

PEPPER

Cucumber Sandwiches

1 8-oz. pkg. cream
cheese, softened
1 pkg. Italian salad dressing mix
party pumpernickel bread
1 cucumber, peeled
and thinly sliced
paprika

Mix the cream cheese and the salad dressing mix. Spread on the bread slices. Add a thin slice of cucumber per piece of bread, then sprinkle with paprika.

Susan Robinson
Mechanicsville, VA

Cucumber Sandwiches

Chapter 3

Salads

Cucumber Salad

3-6 cucumbers
pinch salt
chopped fresh chives
chopped fresh dill
8 oz. sour cream or plain yogurt

Slice the cucumbers very thinly and mix with the salt, chives and dill. Refrigerate for 30 minutes. Mix in the sour cream or yogurt to make a smooth sauce. Garnish with chive flowers.

Yields 4-5 servings.

Renale Rush
Shoals, IN

Cucumber Salad

Confetti Pasta Salad

1 8-oz. pkg. uncooked
shell-shaped pasta
1 cup coarsely chopped broccoli
1 cup coarsely chopped
cauliflower
2 small carrots, sliced
2 T. sliced green onions
1 small bell pepper, cut into
bite-size pieces
1 clove garlic, minced
1/2 tsp. all-purpose seasoning
1/2 cup fat-free Italian
salad dressing
1 tsp. hot sauce (optional)
2 oz. grated Parmesan cheese

Prepare pasta as directed on package. Drain. Cool completely. Combine pasta and ingredients, except the cheese, in a 2-quart bowl. Sprinkle the cheese over the pasta salad.

Makes 8 servings.

HINT: You can add meat to this to make it more hearty. Chicken breasts that are cooked with lemon and pepper and then cut into bite-size pieces are great. Add more dressing if needed.

Rebecca Seehaver
Tuttle, ND

Cucumber Rice Salad

3 cups cooked rice, cooled
2 cups peeled, seeded and
chopped cucumbers
1 small green bell
pepper, chopped
1/2 cup chopped radishes
1 carrot, chopped
3/4 cup frozen peas
1/2 cup Italian dressing
1/2 tsp. dry mustard
1/8 tsp. pepper

Combine the rice, cucumber, green pepper, radishes, carrot and peas. Blend the Italian dressing, dry mustard and pepper. Toss with the rice mixture and chill.

Makes 6 servings.

Doris Melder
Hubertus, WI

Chicken and Rice Salad

1 6-oz. pkg. chicken and
rice mix
2 tsp. butter
1-1/2 tsp. curry powder
1-1/2 cups water
1 boneless, skinless
chicken breast
1 6-oz. jar artichoke
hearts in marinade
10 stuffed green olives, sliced
10 black olives, sliced
1/4 cup sliced green onions
1/4 cup chopped green
bell pepper
1/4 cup mayonnaise

Mix the rice (without the seasoning packet added) and the butter together, and microwave on high for 2 minutes. Stir and cook 1-2 minutes more to brown. Stir in the seasoning packet, the curry powder and the water. Microwave on high for 12-15 minutes, or until just tender, stirring once or twice. Do not overcook. Chill.

Poach the chicken breast until done. Cool and cut into cubes. Drain the artichoke hearts, reserving half of the marinade, and cut them into large pieces. Combine the rice, chicken, artichoke hearts and the remaining ingredients together. Add more mayonnaise, if needed.

Makes five 1/2-cup servings.

Ida R. Turner
Yakima, WA

Carli's Caramel Apple Salad

*1 16-oz. can pineapple,
crushed or tidbits
1/2 cup sugar
1 egg
2 T. all-purpose flour
1/2 tsp. white vinegar
2 cups mini marshmallows
5-1/2 cups chopped
granny smith apples
1 12 oz. container whipped
topping, thawed
1 bag caramels, unwrapped
and cut into squares
6 oz. Spanish peanuts (optional)*

Drain the juice from the pineapple into a saucepan. Add the sugar, egg, flour, and vinegar and whisk together. On medium heat, stir until the mixture has a yucky consistency. Add the marshmallows to the mix and stir until melted. Stir in the pineapples. Let the mixture cool, then refrigerate overnight.

The next day, combine the remaining ingredients in a large serving bowl. Add the pineapple mixture. Keep chilled and enjoy.

Patty Braaten
Richland, WA

Fruit Salad

*1 large pkg. vanilla pudding mix
milk
1 can peaches, cut up
2 cans fruit salad or fruit cocktail
1 can cubed pineapple
3 firm bananas, sliced
red grapes, halved
powdered sugar
1 pt. heavy cream, whipped*

Cook the pudding as directed on the box and cool. Drain the fruit, and put it all in a large bowl. Add powdered sugar to taste, mixing well. Fold in the pudding and cream until well blended. Refrigerate for at least 2 hours before serving.

Lois J. Hart
Johnson City, NY

Virginia's Best Potato Salad

*5 lbs. potatoes
1 cup mayonnaise or
salad dressing
1/2 cup evaporated milk
1/4 cup granulated sugar
2 T. white vinegar
8 large hard-cooked eggs
1 cup chopped onions
1 cup chopped green peppers
1 cup chopped celery
green bell pepper strips
for garnish
Spanish olives for garnish*

In a large cooking pot, boil the potatoes. While they are cooking, mix the mayonnaise, milk, sugar and vinegar together; refrigerate. Peel and finely chop six of the eggs and add to the refrigerated dressing mixture. Slice the other two eggs and save to garnish the salad.

Peel and slice the warm potatoes. Quickly add the refrigerated dressing to potatoes while they are still warm. Stir the potatoes until thoroughly coated with the dressing. Add the chopped vegetables and stir again. Place in a large serving bowl. Level the top of the salad with the back of a large serving spoon and garnish with the sliced eggs, the green pepper strips and the Spanish olives.

Hint: The secret to this recipe is to add the dressing to the potatoes while they are still hot.

Cassy Suess
Jeannette, PA

Radish Slaw

30-40 red radishes, or
4 large Daikon radishes
salt
1 tsp. parsley flakes
2-3 drops vegetable oil
1/2-1 tsp. vinegar
1/2 tsp. celery seed (optional)
1/2 cup finely chopped
onions (optional)

Grate the radishes or shred them in a food processor. Salt generously and let stand for a couple of hours. Drain in to a colander, pressing out as much liquid as possible. Toss the radishes in a large bowl with the rest of the ingredients and serve.

Shellie Johnson
Hornbrook, CA

Radish Slaw

Summer Pasta Salad

1/2 cup red wine vinegar
1/2 cup olive oil
2 T. minced fresh parsley
1 T. minced fresh mint leaves
1 T. minced fresh oregano
1 tsp. minced fresh thyme
1/2 tsp. black pepper
1 T. Dijon mustard
4 cups cooked pasta
(rotini, bows or shells)
1 15-oz. can garbanzo beans
(chick peas), rinsed and drained
8 pepperoncini peppers, chopped
4 plum tomatoes, diced
4 green onions, diced
3 mushrooms, diced
10-12 olives, whole or sliced
1/2 cup crumbled feta cheese

In a large bowl, whisk together the vinegar, oil, herbs and spices. Add the cooked pasta and the remaining ingredients; mix well. Chill for at least 1 hour before serving.

Serves 8-10.

HINT: This is delicious with French bread and iced mint tea.

Rose Veach
Prairie Village, KS

Taco Salad

1 head romaine lettuce, shredded
1 15-oz. can kidney beans,
drained and rinsed
1 1/2 lbs. ground beef, cooked
1-2 large tomatoes, chopped
1 8-oz. pkg. shredded
cheddar cheese
3-4 cups taco chips,
broken small
1 8-oz. bottle Catalina dressing

Combine all of the ingredients, and mix well. Serve immediately.

Serves 12.

Susan Oleson
Gorham, ME

Corn Bread Salad

1 12-oz. pkg. corn bread mix
2 cups buttermilk ranch
    salad dressing
1 15-oz. can whole kernel
    corn, drained
1 cup cubed, fully-cooked ham
1 green bell pepper, chopped
1 tomato, chopped
1 small onion, chopped
3 hard-cooked eggs, chopped
1/4 tsp. salt

Prepare the corn bread mix according to the package directions. Bake as directed, then cool and break into pieces. Combine the corn bread pieces and the remaining ingredients in a large salad bowl. Toss to combine. Cover and chill for 2 hours or longer.

Jean King
Blue Springs, MO

Corn Bread Salad.

Marinated Carrots

1 lb. carrots
1 can tomato soup
1/2 cup sugar
1/2 cup oil
1/2 cup cider vinegar
2 large green bell peppers,
seeded and sliced into rings
2 large onions, sliced
and rings separated

Peel, slice and boil the carrots in water until they are tender. In a small saucepan, combine the soup, sugar, oil and vinegar and bring to a boil. Drain the carrots and combine with the peppers and onions in an airtight container. Pour the soup mixture over the vegetables and refrigerate, stirring several times, until the vegetables are cold.

HINT: This salad will keep its crispiness for several days in the refrigerator.

Teresa Penrod
Wilmington, NC

Marinated Carrots

Tuna Salad

3 cups chopped lettuce
2 6-oz. cans tuna
1 15-oz. can green beans
1 15-oz. can peas
green onions to taste, chopped
2 cups chopped tomatoes
1 cup mayonnaise

Mix all of the ingredients together and serve.

HINT: The mayonnaise should not be added until just before serving, because it tends to get weepy. Chopped green bell peppers and black olives are also good.

Virginia Eichinger
Olathe, KS

Dandelion Greens

young dandelion leaves
3-4 eggs
1/4 cup cider vinegar
1 lb. bacon
5 T. evaporated milk
salt

After picking enough young dandelion leaves to fill a large bowl, soak them and rinse them in cold water. Drain off all of the water, and let leaves sit in a bowl until the dressing is ready.

To make the dressing: Beat the eggs, then mix them with the vinegar. Set aside. Cut the bacon into 1-inch pieces and fry in a large skillet. Drain off 3/4 of the drippings. When the pan is cool, add water until half full, then pour in the egg and vinegar mixture. Heat to a rolling boil, while stirring. Boil for about 30 seconds, then turn off heat. Stir in the milk and taste. Add more vinegar, if needed, and salt to taste. Then immediately pour over the dandelion greens and mix while still hot.

Serve over plain or buttered potato chunks.

HINT: The trick is to get the right amount of vinegar and milk to suit your taste and not to overboil it, or you will scald it and make it bitter.

Darlene Reinoehl
Klingerstown, PA

DANDELION

Italian Potato Salad

3 lbs. red potatoes, cubed
and boiled
1 bunch radishes, sliced
2 cucumbers, sliced
4 stalks celery, chopped
3 ripe tomatoes, cut into wedges
1 medium onion, sliced
salt to taste
pepper to taste
2 T. chopped fresh basil
leaves, or 1 tsp. dried basil
olive oil

Mix the potatoes, radishes, cucumbers, celery, tomatoes and onion. Then add the salt and pepper to taste, and the basil. Add enough oil to moisten salad.

Antionette Piccirillo
Chicago, IL

Italian Potato Salad

Broccoli Salad

1 head broccoli, broken into
small pieces (peel and slice
the stems, as well, and cut
into small pieces)
1/3 cup chopped onion
6 slices bacon, cooked
and crumbled
1 cup broken walnuts
1 cup raisins
1/2 cup mayonnaise
2 T. lemon juice
3 T. sugar
salt
pepper

Combine the broccoli, onion, walnuts, raisins and bacon in a bowl. In a separate bowl, mix the mayonnaise, lemon juice, sugar and lots of salt and pepper. Pour over the salad and serve.

Emma Chaney
Roseville, CA

Hot German Potato Salad

1/2 lb. bacon, cooked
and crumbled
1/2 cup chopped celery
1/2 cup sliced onion
1/4 cup bacon drippings
3 T. sugar
1 T. all-purpose flour
1-1/2 tsp. salt
1/2 tsp. celery seed
1/4 tsp. pepper
1/2 cup water
1/3 cup white vinegar
5 medium potatoes, cooked
and cubed

Cook the bacon until crisp, drain, reserving 1/4 cup of the drippings; crumble the bacon. Sauté the celery and onion in the reserved bacon drippings until tender. Combine the sugar, flour and seasonings and stir into the drippings.

Add the water and vinegar, stirring until smooth. Bring to a boil and add the potatoes and crumbled bacon. Mix thoroughly.

Serves 6.

Cris Samuel
Lexington, SC

Overnight Salad

1 head lettuce, chopped
1/2 cup chopped green onions
1/2 cup chopped celery
1 can sliced water chestnuts
1 10-oz. bag frozen peas
1-1/2 cups mayonnaise, or 3/4
cup mayonnaise and 3/4
cup sour cream
4 oz. cheddar cheese, grated
2 T. sugar
1/2 tsp. salt
3 hard-cooked eggs, finely
chopped
1 can olives, sliced
1/2 lb. bacon, cooked
and crumbled
cherry tomatoes or fancy sliced
tomatoes

Toss the lettuce, green onions, celery, chestnuts and peas together; place half of this mixture in a large bowl. Mix the mayonnaise, cheddar cheese, sugar and salt to form a dressing. Layer half of the dressing on half of the salad, then top with the second half of the salad and a final layer of dressing.

Top the salad with the eggs, olives, bacon and tomatoes. Refrigerate overnight.

Ann Miller
Republic, WA

Cauliflower Broccoli Salad

1 small head cauliflower
4 stalks broccoli
1/4 cup olive oil
2 T. minced onion
2 tsp. grated lemon rind
1 clove garlic, minced
1/2 tsp. sugar
1/4 tsp. paprika
1/8 tsp. pepper
1 clove garlic, whole
1/2 green bell pepper,
   cut in strips
1/2 cup sliced stuffed olives
3 hard-cooked eggs, quartered
2 T. diced pimentos

In a large pan, cook the cauliflower and the broccoli in boiling water until tender-crisp (about 5 minutes). Drain and let the vegetables cool, then separate into flowerettes. In a large bowl, combine the oil, onion, lemon rind, minced garlic, sugar, paprika and pepper. Add the cauliflower and broccoli, tossing to blend. Chill for 30 minutes. Drain the salad, reserving the marinade.

Rub a large bowl with the whole garlic clove. Add the cauliflower, broccoli, green pepper, olives, eggs and pimentos. Pour the reserved marinade over this; toss to coat. Chill for 1-2 hours.

Nadine Standfield
Mounds View, MN

CHAPTER 4

Soups

Chicken Corn Chowder

1 cup diced onions
1 cup butter
4 cups frozen sweet corn
3 cups potatoes, peeled and diced
1-1/2 cups flour
8 cups chicken stock
1 cup light cream
(or half-and-half)
salt
pepper

In a large pot on medium heat, sauté the corn and onions in the butter. When the onions are tender, add the potatoes and flour and stir. Add the chicken stock and stir constantly while bringing to a boil. Reduce heat to a simmer. Cook, stirring occasionally, until the potatoes are tender. Add the cream and salt and pepper to taste. Cook for 10 minutes more.

Denise Leikheim
Schnecksville, PA

Chicken Corn Chowder

Sausage Zucchini Soup

2 lbs. zucchini, sliced
1 lb. hot sausage, sliced
1 lb. mild sausage, sliced
1 cup celery, chopped
1 cup onion, finely chopped
2 16-oz. cans tomatoes, chopped
1 pkg. dry Italian salad dressing
1 10-oz. pkg. frozen corn

Brown the zucchini, sausage, celery and onion in a large pot over medium heat. Then add the rest of the ingredients. Simmer until heated through.

This is delicious served with French bread and sprinkled with Parmesan cheese.

Ginger Heitman
Camp Point, IL

Pumpkin Consommé

1 small to medium pumpkin
1 avocado
fresh sliced wild mushrooms
(optional)
sliced green onions (optional)
chopped chives (optional)
chopped shallots (optional)
squeeze of lime (optional)
cilantro or parsley for garnish

Pumpkin Consommé

Wash the pumpkin and remove the seeds, but do not peel. Cut into 5-10 large pieces and place in a pot with enough water to cover. Heat the water to just under the boiling point and steep for several hours. Place the pumpkin in a colander. Strain the steeping water; return it to the pot. Boil, reducing the water by half to form a consommé.

Meanwhile, scoop the pumpkin from the skin and reserve for other uses. Return 1/2 cup of the scooped pumpkin to the consommé. Peel, pit and slice the avocado. Place several slices in each bowl along with a sprinkling of any combination of optional ingredients.

When the consommé is reduced by half, remove from the heat and strain through a cheesecloth directly into the bowls. Top with chopped cilantro or parsley leaves. Serve with toasted bread.

This makes a great starter course and it can be made up to 6 days in advance. When reheating you can add more pumpkin and strain to serve. This seems to help retain the freshness of flavor.

Anthony Guarino
Seattle, WA

Chicken Chowder

2 strips bacon
1 chicken, cut up
1/4 tsp. ground celery seed
1/4 tsp. poultry seasoning
1 medium onion, chopped
2 stalks celery, chopped
1 medium bell pepper, chopped
4 medium potatoes,
peeled and cubed
3 cups milk
instant mashed potatoes

Cook the bacon until very crisp. Drain on paper towels. Cool and crumble the bacon, then set aside.

Boil the chicken in water to cover with celery seed and poultry seasoning. Remove chicken from the broth, cool and remove skin and bones. Chop chicken and set aside. Simmer vegetables in the broth until tender. Add the chicken and milk to broth. Bring to a boil and thicken with instant mashed potatoes. Stir in bacon bits.

John Grace
Fort Wayne, IN

Sauerkraut Soup

1 lb. spare ribs (pork is best)
1/2 cup uncooked pearl barley
4 medium potatoes,
peeled and diced
2 bay leaves
1 14-oz. can sauerkraut
(do not drain)
salt
pepper

Place the spare ribs and barley in a large kettle. Add water to just cover the ribs. Boil until meat is tender. When tender you can remove the meat from the bones. Discard bones and return meat to pot. Add the potatoes and the bay leaves; simmer until tender. Add the sauerkraut and salt and pepper to taste. (If the sauerkraut is added before the potatoes are done, the potatoes with have a crust on them.) Turn the heat down and simmer for 30 minutes.

Janice Turnmire
Bangor, WI

Cream of Lettuce Soup

1/4 cup butter
1/4 cup flour
1/2 tsp. salt
4 cups milk
2 beef bouillon cubes (or 2 tsp.
beef soup base)
1/4 tsp. fresh onion juice
4 cups slightly packed finely
shredded lettuce
1/4 cup finely diced radishes

In the top of a double boiler, melt butter. Stir in flour and salt and cook for 2 minutes. Whisk in milk. Cook until thickened, stirring occasionally to keep smooth. Add the bouillon cubes and the onion juice; stir well. Add the lettuce; boil for 10 minutes. Just before serving, sprinkle the radishes over each bowlful. Serve promptly.

Makes 4 servings.

Suzanne Johnston
Marinette, WI

String Bean Soup

1 lb. fresh string beans, snapped
into 1-inch pieces
water
1 cup peeled and diced potatoes
1 medium onion, chopped
1 T. butter
1 T. flour
1 cup milk
fresh bacon bits for garnish

In a large saucepan, cover the beans with water and start to cook over medium heat while you prepare the potatoes. Add the potatoes and let the beans continue to cook with the potatoes until they are both tender. In a soup pot, sauté the onion in the butter until tender. Add the flour and mix until bubbly. Blend in the milk slowly. After the white sauce thickens, add the water from the vegetables. Last, stir in the cooked vegetables. Garnish with bacon bits.

HINT: Chicken bouillon granules can be added after the milk. Try seasoning with garlic and onion powder, or dill and parsley.

Joyce G. McGuire
Elkhart, IN

Grandmother Paasch's Grape Soup

3 6-oz. cans grape
juice concentrate
10 cans water
2 cooking apples, cored,
peeled and cubed
1/4 cup sugar
4 sticks cinnamon
3 cups milk
2 eggs
2-3 cups, plus 3 heaping T.
all-purpose flour
dash salt

Mix the grape juice, water, apples, sugar and cinnamon in a large saucepan; simmer for about 1 hour. Meanwhile prepare the dumplings. Combine the milk and 3 T. flour in a saucepan. Boil and stir until the mixture pulls away from the sides of the pan. Let it cool then beat in the eggs, salt, and enough flour to make it very stiff.

Drop the dumpling mixture into the soup by the teaspoonful. (Dip the spoon in the soup before spooning each dumpling, so it will slide off the spoon.) Cover and simmer for 10 minutes. Turn off the heat and let stand for another 10 minutes.

HINT: We always have one test dumpling. If it dissolves (cooks up), add more flour.

Chesmond Bade
Eaton, OH

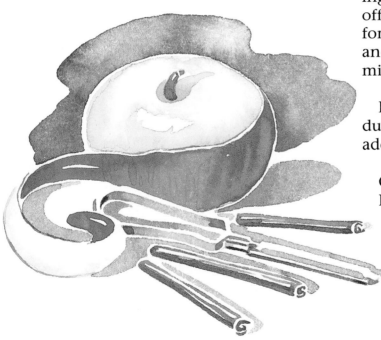

Early Spring Soup

1-1/2 lbs. beef, cut into cubes
7 cups water
1 large onion, chopped
1 large carrot, sliced
1 lb. potatoes, peeled and diced
1 cup chopped celery
2 10-oz pkgs. fresh spinach,
thinly sliced
1 tsp. salt (optional)
2 bay leaves
sour cream or plain
yogurt for garnish
chopped hard-boiled
eggs for garnish

In a soup kettle, combine the beef and the water, and bring to a boil over medium-high heat. Reduce the heat, cover and simmer for 1-1/2 to 2 hours, or until the meat is tender. Add the onion, carrot, potatoes and celery. Cover and simmer for 25 minutes more, or until the vegetables are tender. Add the remaining ingredients except garnishes, and bring to a boil. Boil for 2 minutes.

Serve the soup in bowls and top each one with a heaping tablespoon of sour cream or plain yogurt, and a tablespoon of chopped hard-boiled egg.

Larisa Logan
Spokane, WA

Tortellini Soup

1-1/2 lbs. mild Italian
sausage, crumbled
2 cloves garlic, minced
1 large onion, chopped
2 15-oz. cans Italian
stewed tomatoes
2 15-oz. cans beef broth
1 1/2 cups dry red wine
1 red or green bell
pepper, chopped
2 small zucchini, sliced
1 lb. sliced fresh mushrooms
1 pkg. cheese tortellini
3 T. chopped fresh parsley
1/2 tsp. dry basil leaves

Brown the sausage with the garlic and onions in large pot; drain. Add the tomatoes, broth and wine; simmer for 30 minutes. Add the vegetables, noodles and herbs; simmer until tender. Serve with garlic bread.

Carol Krog
Eddyville, OR

Pea Soup

6 cups hot water
1 bag dried split peas
1 ham bone
1 large carrot, peeled and sliced
2 medium celery sticks, cut into
large sections
1 medium onion, sliced
2 cloves garlic, minced
2 large bay leaves
1/2 tsp. dry thyme
pinch cumin seeds

Put all of the ingredients into a large pot and bring to a boil. Reduce the heat and let it simmer for 1 hour, or until the peas are cooked to a mush. Remove the ham bone, bay leaves and celery sticks. Puree soup in a blender or food processor. Reheat, if necessary.

Marie L. Gauthier
North Smithfield, RI

Mint Soup

12-15 *fresh mint leaves,*
stems included
small handful fresh
parsley, chopped
2 *large onions, chopped*
1 *clove garlic, minced*
1 *celery, cut into small pieces*

Put all ingredients, except the celery, into a large stockpot. Add water until it is 3/4 full. Bring to a boil, then reduce to a low simmer. Simmer for 3-6 hours, stirring occasionally (the longer it simmers the better it is). Add the celery pieces and cook for 30 minutes more.

This soup freezes very well.

Chana Glanstein
Far Rockaway, NY

Mint Soup

Summer's End Stew

1-1/2 lbs. beef stew meat, cubed
1 T. vegetable oil
8-12 fresh tomatoes,
peeled and cut up
2 cups tomato juice or water
2 medium onions, chopped
1 clove garlic, minced
2 tsp. salt
1/2 tsp. pepper
4-6 small potatoes,
peeled and quartered
3-5 carrots, sliced
2 cups corn
2 cups green beans, cut up
2 cups peas
2-3 stalks celery, sliced
1 cup cut up summer squash
1/4 cup snipped fresh parsley
1 tsp. sugar

In a Dutch oven, brown the meat in oil over medium-high heat. Add the tomatoes, tomato juice or water, onions, garlic, salt and pepper. Bring to a boil then reduce the heat, and simmer for 1 hour.

Add the potatoes, carrots, corn, green beans, peas and celery. Cover and simmer for 30 minutes. Add the squash and simmer for 10-15 minutes, or until the meat and vegetables are all tender. Stir in the parsley and the sugar.

This stew is perfect for using up those last vegetables in the garden. Substitute with whatever you have left growing.

Makes 16 servings.

Anna Farmer
Hot Springs, AR

Summer's End Stew

Slow Cooker Deer Stew

2 T. vegetable shortening
2 lbs. deer tenderloin, cubed
2 T. ground pepper, divided
1 T. minced garlic
3 cups water
1 medium onion,
coarsely chopped
1 cup fresh green beans,
cut into 1-inch pieces
4 medium potatoes, coarsely cut
1 cup fresh corn,
removed from cob
1 cup fresh tomatoes,
coarsely cut
2 T. chopped fresh parsley

Heat the vegetable shortening in a frying pan. When the shortening is hot, add the cubed deer meat, 1 T. pepper and the garlic. Brown the meat on all sides. Place the meat in a slow cooker. Add the remaining ingredients, cover and turn slow cooker on high. Cook for 8 hours and serve.

Sandra Burgess
Bucktree, MO

Hearty Down-Home Garden Stew

1 cup thinly sliced garden carrots
1 cup garden potatoes, diced
2-1/2 T. margarine
1 cup garden green bell
pepper, diced
1 cup garden red bell
pepper, diced
1 cup garden yellow onion, diced
2 cloves garlic, minced
1 lb. lean ground beef
(or ground turkey), crumbled
1/4 cup all-purpose flour
2 large garden tomatoes,
peeled and diced
2 cups hot water
1/3 cup dry sherry
1/4 cup honey barbecue sauce
1 tsp beef base
1 tsp. dried summer savory
1 tsp. dried basil

Pre-cook the carrots and potatoes. In a 4-qt. pan, melt the margarine over medium heat. Add the peppers, onion and garlic. Cook until tender. Add the beef and brown evenly, stirring occasionally. Stir in the flour; cook for 15 minutes. Add the tomatoes and mix well. Add the water, sherry, barbecue sauce, beef base, summer savory and basil. Cook for 30 minutes on medium-low heat, stirring occasionally. Add the carrots and potatoes; cook for 20 minutes more.

This stew can be served over rice, or just by itself.

Makes 6-8 servings.

Florence A. Hite
Berkeley Springs, WV

B A S I L

Chili

1 large onion, chopped
1 T. vegetable oil
2-3 lbs. hamburger or
ground chuck, crumbled
2 tsp. chili powder, divided
salt to taste
pepper to taste
1 15-oz. can crushed tomatoes
(home canned are best)
2 15-oz. cans dark
red kidney beans
2 15-oz. cans light
red kidney beans
2 15-oz. cans hot chili beans
1 8-oz. can tomato sauce

Sauté the onion in oil in a large skillet. Add the crumbled hamburger, 1 teaspoon chili powder and the salt and pepper. Cook until the hamburger is done, then drain well.

In a large soup kettle, combine all canned ingredients and one bean can full of water. Bring to a boil. Add the hamburger mixture and the remaining 1 teaspoon chili powder. Reduce heat and simmer for 1-2 hours.

Joyce A. Maynard
Oakwood, VA

Crab Meat Artichoke Soup

1 bunch green onions, chopped
1 T. margarine
3 10-1/2-oz. cans
cream of mushroom soup
3 10-1/2-oz. cans
cream of celery soup
3 10-1/2-oz. cans chopped
artichoke hearts in water, drained
3 12-1/2-oz. cans
evaporated milk
1 lb. crab meat, flaked
1/2 tsp. Worcestershire sauce
1/4 tsp. cayenne pepper

Sauté the green onions in margarine, then add the remaining ingredients and simmer, covered, until flavors are blended (15-20 minutes).

Sylvia A. Damare
Slidell, LA

Beef Stew Par Excellence

2 lbs. boneless stew beef, cubed
1 1/2 lbs. bone-in beef brisket
potatoes, cut into medium slices
carrots, sliced
celery, sliced
onions, sliced
1 T. dry sherry
1 T. salt
1 bay leaf
1/2 tsp. black pepper
1/2 tsp. paprika
1/4 tsp. ground marjoram

In a large stockpot, combine the stew beef and the brisket; add water to cover. Bring to a boil. Reduce heat and simmer for 1 1/2 hours. Remove the bone from the brisket, cut up meat, and return it to pot.

Add the vegetables in desired quantities and the seasonings, mixing thoroughly. Cook over medium heat for about 2 hours or until all of the vegetables and meat are tender and broth is rich and succulent, stirring occasionally.

Serve with your favorite bread, and for an additional tangy taste, Tabasco sauce.

Jimmy E. Howard
Arab, AL

Ann's Down Home Potato Soup

6-8 medium red potatoes,
peeled and cubed
8 cups water
1 lb. country smoked
sausage, thinly sliced
2 12-oz. cans evaporated milk
1/2 cup flour
1/4 cup margarine, softened
1 pkg. sliced ham, cubed
1 bunch green onions, chopped
salt
black pepper

In a 4 1/2-qt. Dutch oven or soup kettle, boil the potatoes in 8 cups water until almost tender. Drain, reserving the potato water. Sauté the sausage in a skillet over medium-low heat until well done. Drain on paper towels.

Return the potato water to the soup kettle. Add the evaporated milk and cook over medium to low heat until the mixture is thoroughly heated. Mix the flour with the margarine and add to the kettle, stirring until well blended. Add the potatoes, sausage, ham and green onions. Blend well. Salt and pepper to taste. Cook on low for about 2 hours, stirring occasionally. You may need to add a little more water to achieve the correct consistency.

HINT: You may use julienned chicken in place of the ham or sausage.

Dorothy Ann Stundivant
McComb, MS

Easy Minestrone

1 large onion, chopped
1 cup sliced celery
1/2 tsp. garlic powder
2 T. vegetable oil
4 10-oz. cans condensed
  beef broth
16 oz. Italian plum tomatoes
  (fresh or canned)
1 20-oz. can white great
  Northern beans
16 oz. Italian green beans
  (fresh or frozen)
16 oz. peas and carrots
  (fresh or frozen)
1/2 cup uncooked
  elbow macaroni
1/2 tsp. dried oregano
1/4 tsp. pepper
  salt

Sauté the onion, celery and garlic powder in the oil. Add the remaining ingredients. Bring to a slow boil over medium-high. Reduce heat, cover and simmer for 45 minutes.

Serves 8.

Lynne Larkee-Allen
Neenah, WI

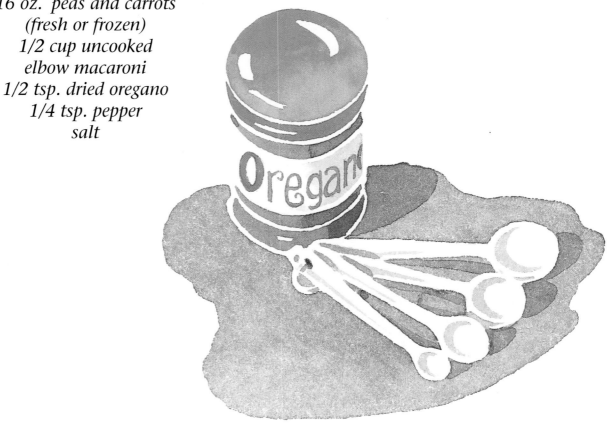

Pinky Dink Soup

2 cups beef broth
3 cups water
1 cup green beans, cut up
1 cup peas
1 cup corn
1 cup uncooked macaroni
1/2 cup diced carrots
1/2 cup sliced celery
1/4 cup diced onion
1/2 cup beets

Combine all of the ingredients in a big soup pot and bring to a boil over high heat. Reduce the heat and simmer for 1 1/2-2 hours, stirring occasionally. The soup becomes a thick stew when done.

Kim Kasch
Portland, OR

Chicken and Rice Soup

1 lb. boneless, skinless
chicken breast
1 heart of celery, chopped
1 medium onion, chopped
4-5 large carrots, sliced
3 cups water
1 14-1/2-oz. can chicken broth
or broth from 1 whole chicken
2 tsp. black pepper
1 tsp. minced garlic
1 tsp. celery salt
salt
2 cups cooked white rice

Cook the chicken in the oven at 375° until done, then cut into bite-size pieces. Place the chicken pieces in a 4-qt. pot. Add celery, onion, carrots, water and chicken broth. Over medium heat, cook until it comes to a rolling boil. Reduce heat to a simmer, and add the pepper, garlic, celery salt and salt to taste. Continue simmering until the celery and carrots are tender. Add the cooked rice and cook 10 minutes more.

This soup is best when cooked the night before and refrigerated.

Serves 4-5.

Lorie Linton
St. Charles, IL

Split Pea Soup With Herbs

1 lb. dried split peas
1 lb. beef sausage
2 carrots, chopped
1 potato, diced
1/2 cup diced onions
2 tsp. salt
1/2 tsp. smoke salt (optional)
1/2 tsp. dried basil
1/2 tsp. dried rosemary
1/2 tsp. dried summer savory
1/4 tsp. dried marjoram
1/4 tsp. dried thyme
1/4 tsp. dried sage
1 bay leaf
8 cups water

Soak the split peas in water to cover for 4 hours and then drain. Brown the sausage in the soup pot and then remove; set aside. Put the peas and the remaining ingredients into the pot. Add the 8 cups water. Simmer covered for 2 hours.

If you like the soup smooth, you can purée it all at this point, otherwise just purée the vegetables. Add the sausage and simmer for 30 minutes. You may need to add more water to thin soup, if desired.

Serve with croutons.

Susan Brand
Nyack, NY

CHAPTER 5

Main Dishes

Dajaj Muhammar (Roasted Chicken)

2 cloves of garlic, minced
1 tsp. mild curry powder
1 tsp. hot curry powder
1 tsp. fresh oregano
1 tsp. fresh thyme
1 tsp. fresh basil
3/4 tsp. salt
3/4 tsp. pepper
1 tsp. fresh tarragon
1/2 tsp. minced fresh ginger
1/2 tsp. cumin
1/2 tsp. paprika
1/2 fresh lemon juice
4-5 lbs. chicken, cut up
1/2 cup olive oil
1/2 cup dry red wine
1/2 cup chicken broth

Blend herb ingredients together. In a large bowl combine chicken and olive oil, turning to coat chicken. Add herb mix, coating every piece of chicken with that mixture.

Put the chicken in a square or round pan (brush the pan with olive oil), then add the wine and the broth. Preheat oven to 350°. Cover the chicken with foil and bake for 1 hour. Uncover and bake another 1/2 hour. When the chicken is brown and tender, it is done.

Bon appetit!

Carlos Judeh
Anaheim, CA

Djaj Muhammar (Rosasted Chicken)

Chicken Cutlets Scallopini

*1 lb. boneless, skinless
chicken breasts
2 egg whites, slightly beaten
1/2 cup seasoned bread crumbs
1/4 cup margarine
8 oz. mushrooms, thinly sliced
1 medium onion, thinly sliced
1 medium green bell
pepper, thinly sliced
1/4 cup dry sherry
1 T. water
1 tsp. dried basil leaves*

Pound chicken breasts to 1/4" thickness. Coat cutlets alternately with beaten egg and bread crumbs. Melt margarine in large skillet over medium heat. Sauté thinly sliced mushrooms, onion and bell pepper until tender – don't overcook. Remove from pan.

Sauté the cutlets in remaining margarine, a few pieces at a time until browned. Remove from pan. Add sherry and water to pans. Return the mushrooms, onion, pepper and chicken. Sprinkle with basil. Serve with your favorite pasta.

Serves 4.

Thomas C. Michael
Golf Breeze, FL

Tortilla Pie

1 lb. ground beef
1 pkg. corn tortillas
1 15-oz. can whole kernel corn,
    drained
1 onion, chopped
1 small can green chilies
12 oz. cheddar cheese, shredded
1 15-oz. can chili

Brown the beef in a skillet and drain. Place a layer of tortillas in the bottom of a 2-quart casserole dish. Put a layer of meat, corn, chopped onion, green chilies and cheese. Repeat until you run out of ingredients. Pour chili over top and top with cheese. Bake at 350° until cheese melts.

Sara Adcock
Abilene, TX

Ground Meat and Cabbage Casserole

1 lb. ground meat, lightly browned and drained
1 small cooked cabbage (chopped and drained)
1 cup sour cream
1/2 cup grated cheese
1 tsp. salt
dash pepper
bread crumbs

Mix the browned meat, chopped cabbage, sour cream, cheese, salt and pepper in a bowl. Put all into a lightly greased, ovenproof dish. Sprinkle bread crumbs on top. Bake in a 350° oven for 30 minutes, or until it bubbles around edges. Serve hot.

Elzie Peacook
Louisville, KY

Potatoes and Knuckles

4 medium potatoes, peeled,
cut into quarters
2 cups all-purpose flour
1 egg
1/4 cup milk
pinch salt
1 lb. lean bacon, diced
1 large onion, chopped
1/4 cup paprika
1 cup milk
sour cream
salt to taste

Add potatoes to 4 quarts boiling, salted water. Cook until partially done. Do not drain. Combine flour, egg, 1/4 cup milk and a pinch of salt to form a firm dough. Roll out to about 1/8" thick, cut into squares about the size of your palm. Pinch off pieces about the size of a quarter into the potato water. Cook "knuckles" until tender. Drain, but save the water.

Fry bacon and onion in a saucepan. Drain some of the grease. Drizzle some grease over the knuckles to avoid sticking. Add paprika, to bacon-onion mixture. Stir. Slowly add about half of the reserved potato water to mixture. Add milk.

Serve Potatoes and Knuckles in large bowls. Top with sour cream. Enjoy.

Patches Didier
Zephryrhills, FL

Macaroni and Cheese with Tomato

2 cups elbow macaroni
(cook 10 minutes in boiling,
salted water – drain)
4 T. butter
1/4 cup all-purpose flour
1 tsp. crumbled oregano
1 tsp. salt
1/4 tsp. pepper
2 cups milk
2 cups shredded cheddar cheese
3-4 medium tomatoes, peeled
and sliced
2 T. butter
1 cup soft bread crumbs
1/2 tsp. dried oregano

Melt butter in a saucepan. Stir in flour, oregano, salt and pepper. Gradually blend in milk. Cook until thickened. Remove from stove and add cheese. Stir until smooth. Add macaroni; mix well.

In 2 1/2-quart baking dish, arrange tomatoes alternately with macaroni and cheese sauce. Reserve 4 or 5 slices of tomato for top.

Melt butter; stir in bread crumbs and oregano. Sprinkle around edges of dish. Decorate top with 4 or 5 slices of tomato.

Bake at 350° oven for 30 minutes, or until bubbly and light brown. Enjoy!

Helen Hasto
Cobleskill, NY

Stuffed Peppers

*2 lbs. lean ground
chuck or turkey
1 cup uncooked rice
(any variety)
2 eggs
1 clove garlic, minced
2 large bell peppers,
sliced in half, seeded
2 qts. vegetable juice
2 T. sugar
salt and pepper to taste*

Combine meat, rice, eggs and garlic in large bowl . Fill the bell pepper halves with mixture. Form any remaining mixture into large balls.

Place peppers and balls into large pot. Pour juice over peppers. Sprinkle with sugar, salt and pepper.

Simmer over medium heat for 1/2 hour or until tender. Juice will thicken as it cooks.

Serve over homemade noodles. Get ready for the compliments!

Patches Didier
Zephyrhills, FL

Al's Presto Pesto

1 10-oz. pkg. frozen
chopped spinach, thawed
1 cup water
1 tsp. black pepper
(fresh ground preferred)
1/2 tsp. hot pepper flakes
2 peeled garlic cloves
1 cup fresh basil
(or 2 T. dried basil)
1 cup fresh parsley
(or 3 T. dried parsley)
1 T. grated fresh
Parmesan cheese
2 T. olive oil
1/4 cup pine nuts or chopped
walnuts (optional)

In blender or food processor, blend spinach, water, pepper, pepper flakes and garlic for 1 minute. Add basil, parsley and cheese; blend for 1 minute. Add oil; blend for 30 seconds. Add nuts and blend until finely chopped.

Serve over your favorite hot cooked pasta.

Alfred LoCascio
West Haven, CT

Al's Presto Pesto

Eggplant Stuffed Bell Peppers

Meat mixture:

1 lb. ground chuck
1 large yellow onion, chopped
1/2 cup Italian bread crumbs
1/2 cup water
1 egg
1/4 cup chopped celery
1/4 cup chopped green onions
1/4 cup Parmesan cheese
1/4 cup chopped green pepper
1/4 tsp. white pepper
1/4 tsp. garlic powder
1/4 tsp. minced garlic
1/2 tsp.garlic juice
1/4 tsp. season-all
1/2 t.meat tenderizer
1 clove of garlic, chopped
1 box corn bread stuffing
1 large eggplant
8-10 bell peppers, tops sliced
off and seeds removed

Preheat oven to 375°.

In large bowl, combine all meat mixture ingredients. Brown mixture in frying pan on low flame until no longer pink. Take off heat and set aside.

Prepare stuffing according to directions (for moist stuffing); mix with meat. Peel and dice eggplant. Boil 10 minutes in salted water. Mash and mix into meat mixture. Stuff mixture into peppers. Bake in a shallow baking dish with an inch of water for 45 minutes to 1 hour.

Serves 8 to 10.

Sahatrice Theresa Inzliageglio
Chalmette, LA

Spinach and Rice (Greek Recipe)

1 lb. cubed lamb with
fat trimmed off
2 medium onions, chopped
1 large can tomatoes, squashed
1 cup water
salt and pepper to taste
2 10-oz. pkgs. frozen spinach
1 cup uncooked rice
1 lemon

Lightly brown lamb in bottom of Dutch oven or large pan with lid. Add chopped onions. Add tomatoes and water, cook 10 minutes. Lay frozen spinach on top of mixture. Break up spinach as it cooks. Add rice, salt and pepper, and cook, covered, until rice is done. Top with juice of lemon. Serve with corn bread. NOTE: Ground hamburger can be used instead of lamb.

David McGowan
Pt. Pleasant, WV

Zucchini Quiche

6 cups diced zucchini
1 1/2 cups biscuit mix
1 cup grated cheese of choice
1 onion, grated
5 eggs, beaten
1/2 cup vegetable oil
1 small can mushrooms, drained
parsley, salt, pepper to taste
4-6 sticks bacon, fried and
crumbled (optional)

Combine all ingredients in a big bowl. Pour into a large, greased pie dish. Bake at 350° for 40-50 minutes, until lightly brown. Happy Cooking!

Laura Luther
New Florence, PA

Hungarian Delite

*1 lb. beef, cut into 1/2 to
1 inch cubes
2 medium onions, minced
2 T. brown sugar
1-1/4 tsp. paprika
1-1/4 tsp. salt
1/4 tsp. dry mustard
6 T. ketchup (I use lite ketchup)
3 T. Worcestershire sauce
3/4 tsp. cider vinegar
1-1/2 cups water
3 T. all-purpose flour
1 6-oz. pkg. egg noodles*

Brown meat in large pot and add onions. Combine brown sugar, paprika, salt and mustard in a bowl. Combine ketchup, Worcestershire sauce and vinegar in another bowl. Add this mixture to the mustard mixture. Add to meat pot with 1 cup of water and stir well, cover and cook over low heat for 3-1/2 hours or until meat is very tender. Blend flour with remaining 1/2 cup of water and add to meat mixture at end of cooking time. Stir until liquid has thickened.

Prepare noodles as directed on package. Serve meat mixture over noodles. Makes about 4 to 6 servings.

NOTE: I have a pressure cooker and use it to tenderize the meat before I add any other ingredients. This cuts preparation time to only about 1-1/2 hours.

Elaine Asher
Jacksonville, FL

Halibut Supreme with Cheese Dill Sauce

1 lb. halibut fillets (or steaks)
1/2 cup white wine
2 T. butter, melted
1 tsp. garlic powder
1 tsp. white pepper
1 cup sour cream
1/2 cup cheddar cheese, grated
1 T. garlic, minced
1 T. chopped fresh dill
(or 1 tsp. dry dill)
1/2 cup cooked bay shrimp

Preheat oven to 450°. Place fillets in a shallow baking pan. Add wine, butter, garlic powder and white pepper. Bake for 6-7 minutes, or until fish flakes easily. Do not overbake. Meanwhile, combine sour cream, cheese, garlic and dill in saucepan over low heat. Simmer until cheese melts; keep warm. Remove fish from oven, top with cheese sauce and shrimp.

Tip: A must for frozen halibut! Sure to please everyone. I highly recommend the cheese sauce for any white fish.

G.J. Seffelaan
Broadview, Saskatchewan

Eggplant - Tomato - Zucchini Pasta

1/4 cup olive oil
1 eggplant, peeled and cubed
(about 1 1/2 cups)
2 medium zucchini, cubed
(about 2 cups)
1 medium onion, chopped
1 clove garlic, minced
1 lb. tomatoes, seeded
and chopped
1/2 cup chopped parsley
1/2 tsp. dried basil
1 T. Worcestershire sauce
1/2 tsp. Tabasco
salt and pepper to taste

Heat a Dutch oven or heavy skillet over medium heat. Add olive oil; sauté eggplant in oil until soft and browned all over. Remove with a slotted spoon, and set aside. Add more oil to skillet as necessary and sauté zucchini. Remove and set aside. Sauté onion and garlic until tender.

Add tomatoes to the onion and reduce heat to simmer. Add the parsley, Worcestershire sauce, basil, Tabasco, salt and pepper. If the tomatoes are tart, add a teaspoon of sugar. Return the eggplant and the zucchini to the skillet and simmer until heated through. Adjust the seasoning, if necessary. Serve over a bed of cooked thin spaghetti.

Roxanna Francesconi
Shelbyville, TN

Shrimp and Pasta Stir Fry

1/2 lb. medium fresh
unpeeled shrimp
1/4 cup nonfat mayonnaise
1/4 cup chicken broth
1 tsp. grated lemon rind
1 T. fresh lemon juice
1 cup diagonally sliced fresh
asparagus(1-inch lengths)
vegetable cooking spray
2 tsp. vegetable oil
1 T. grated, peeled gingerroot
2 cloves garlic, minced
1/4 tsp. lemon pepper
2 cups hot cooked penne pasta

Peel and devein shrimp; set aside. Combine mayonnaise, broth, lemon peel and lemon juice in a bowl; stir well with a wire whisk, and set aside.

Coat a wok or large nonstick skillet with cooking spray; add oil and place over medium-high heat until hot. Add asparagus, gingerroot and garlic; stir-fry 1 minute. Add shrimp; stir-fry 3 minutes, or until shrimp is done. Stir in mayonnaise mixture and pasta; cook until thoroughly heated. Sprinkle with lemon pepper.

Julie Gant
Macungie, PA

Easy Cheesy Pasta Sauce

2 medium tomatoes
1 small onion
1 small bell pepper
10 oz. cheddar cheese, cubed
hot cooked pasta

Chop tomatoes and onion into small chunks. Cut bell peppers into strips. In a saucepan, melt cheddar cheese over low heat. Add tomatoes, onion and pepper. Mix and cook for 3 minutes. Pour over pasta. Garnish with fresh parsley.

Rose Flynn
Wildwood, NJ

Grilled Basil Chicken

3 T. lemon juice
2 tsp. dried basil
1 clove garlic
1/4 cup olive oil
4 boneless, skinless chicken
breast halves

Combine lemon juice, dried basil and garlic in blender. Blend for 30 seconds. Gradually add olive oil while blending. Brush chicken with half of the basil mixture and refrigerate 30 minutes. Grill chicken for 30 minutes, basting while grilling.

Linette Graham
Naperville, IL

Grilled Chicken

2 chickens, halved
2 garlic cloves, halved
1/4 cup vegetable oil
2 T. white vinegar
1 T. Worcestershire sauce
2 tsp. lime juice
1 tsp. garlic salt
1 tsp. sugar or honey
1/2 tsp. paprika
any of your favorite herbs: chives,
lemon verbena, Greek oregano,
thyme, rosemary, basil, summer
savory, etc.

Rub halved chickens with freshly cut garlic cloves. Place chickens in a shallow glass dish. Combine remaining ingredients and blend well; pour over chicken. Marinate 2 hours in refrigerator, turning once. Drain, saving marinade. Grill chickens over medium heat, skin side up, until no longer pink and juices run clear, turning and basting often.

Sharon McCarney
Battle Lake, MN

Sukiyaki

2 T. vegetable oil
1-1/2 lbs. steak, cut into
    very thin strips
3/4 cup soy sauce
1/4 cup sugar
1/4 cup water, or vegetable stock
2 medium onions, sliced
1 green pepper, sliced into
    thin strips
1 cup celery, cut into
    1-1/2" pieces
1 can bamboo shoots, cut
    into thin strips
1 can mushrooms
1 bunch green onions, cut
    into 1" lengths
1 pkg. tofu (bean curd), cubed
Shirataki (yam threads, look
    like rubber bands!)

Heat oil in skillet over medium-high heat. Add meat and brown lightly. Combine soy sauce, sugar and water. Stir-fry half of this with the meat. Push meat to one side of the pan and add onions, green pepper and celery. Stir-fry for a few minutes. Add remaining soy sauce, the bamboo shoots and mushrooms. Cook a few minutes more and add green onions. Continue to cook, adding the tofu and Shirataki. (Sake may also be added, if desired.) Stir and serve immediately over hot rice.

Ernest Snider
Buffalo, NY

Fool Proof Manicotti

*10 oz. fresh (or thawed and
drained) chopped broccoli
1 cup shredded cooked chicken
1/2 cup large curd cottage
cheese, drained
1/2 cup grated Parmesan cheese
10 manicotti shells
1 egg, beaten
2 10-1/2-oz. cans condensed
cream of chicken soup
16 oz. sour cream
2 cups of milk
1/4 cup dried onion flakes
1/2 tsp. Italian seasoning
1/2 tsp. herb blend
1 cup boiling water
1 cup shredded colby-jack cheese
2 T. chopped fresh parsley*

Combine broccoli, chicken, cottage cheese, Parmesan and egg in bowl. Spoon about 1/4 cup of filling in each uncooked shell. Arrange in 13 x 9"-inch baking dish so they are not touching each other.

Combine soup, sour cream, milk, onion flakes and seasonings. Pour over filled manicotti shells. Pour boiling water carefully around edges of baking dish. Cover tightly with foil. Bake at 350° for 1 hour. Pull back foil and add cheese and parsley. Cover and let stand 5 minutes.

Jami Boan
Independence, MO

Eggplant Parmesan

2 T. all-purpose flour
eggplant
1/3 cup egg substitute
2 T. milk
2/3 cup dry breadcrumbs
1/2 tsp. Italian seasoning
1 medium onion, chopped
1 each green bell and red bell
pepper, chopped
3 large carrots, shredded
2 T. butter
2 large cans chopped tomatoes
Italian seasoning to taste
2 T. red wine vinegar
1 6-oz. can tomato
paste (optional)
Italian sausage (optional)
bay leaf
1 8-oz. pkg. shredded
mozzarella cheese

To prepare the eggplant: Place flour in a large sealable bag; set aside. Peel and cut eggplant into 1/2" thick slices. Place slices in bag; shake to coat. Combine egg substitute and milk; set aside. Combine breadcrumbs and 1/2 teaspoon Italian seasoning. Dip each eggplant slice into egg mixture then dredge lightly in breadcrumbs. Place slices on baking sheet coated with cooking spray. Bake at 400° for 6 - 8 minutes on each side, or until lightly browned.

To prepare the marinara sauce: In a heavy saucepan, sauté onion, peppers and carrots in butter over medium heat until soft or slightly brown. Pour in tomatoes, with juice. Add Italian seasoning and bay leaf. Bring sauce to a boil, then simmer for 30 minutes, stirring occasionally to prevent sticking. Add red wine vinegar. Thicken with tomato paste if necessary. If desired, brown Italian sausage, drain, slice, and add to sauce for flavor.

To assemble the Eggplant Parmesan: Line bottom of 9 x 13-inch greased baking dish with a layer of eggplant slices. Top with a layer of marinara sauce. Repeat. Top with shredded mozzarella cheese. Bake in 400° oven 20 to 30 minutes, or until bubbling and hot.

Serves 8.

Sheri Dorn
Blacksburg, VA

Fancy Egg Scramble

1-1/2 cups diced
Canadian bacon
1/4 cup chopped green onions
3 T. butter
12 eggs, beaten
4 tsp. butter, melted
2-1/4 cups soft breadcrumbs
1/8 tsp. paprika
2 T. melted butter
2 T. all-purpose flour
1/2 tsp. salt
1/8 pepper
2 cups milk
1 cup shredded processed
American cheese

Melt 2 tablespoons butter over medium heat and blend in flour, salt and pepper. Add milk; cook and stir until bubbly. Stir in American cheese until melted. Set cheese sauce aside. In large skillet, cook bacon and onions in the 3 T. butter over medium heat until onions are tender but not brown. Add eggs and scramble just until set. Fold cooked eggs into cheese sauce. Spoon into a 12 x 7"-inch baking dish. Combine melted butter, crumbs and paprika; sprinkle over eggs. Cover; chill until 30 minutes before serving. Bake, uncovered at 350° for 30 minutes.

Phyliss Goodrich
Reseda, CA

Japanese Tomato Beef

2 T. vegetable oil
2 small onions, cut into wedges
1 green bell pepper, diced
1 lb. sirloin steak, sliced
into thin strips
2 16-oz. cans chopped tomatoes
(or 1 qt. of your own
home canned tomatoes)
1/4 cup ketchup
1 T. soy sauce
2 T. sugar
1 tsp. salt
dash pepper
2 T. cornstarch, mixed in
1/2 cup cold water

In a large fry pan, sauté onions and green pepper in oil over medium-high heat until partially cooked. Add steak strips and stir-fry. When steak is browned, add tomatoes, ketchup, soy sauce, sugar, salt and pepper. When mixture is boiling, stir in cornstarch and water. Continue stirring until thickened. Serve over steamed white rice.

Jodie Stevenson
Export, PA

Braciolla

round steak
salt
pepper
fresh parsley
fresh chopped garlic
fresh grated Parmesan cheese
olive oil
spaghetti sauce

Pound one slice of round steak until 1/4" thick. Season with spices to taste and roll as you would a jelly roll. Secure with toothpicks. Brown all sides of roll in olive oil in a skillet. Cook at 350° in a casserole dish with spaghetti sauce for 2 hours.

Crystal Reformat
Wheatfield, IN

Cranberry Chicken

4 slices bacon
2-1/2 to 3 lbs. chicken, cut up
1 jar small whole onions, drained
green beans (optional)
mushrooms (optional)
1 pkg. onion soup mix
16-oz. can whole-berry
cranberry sauce
1/3 cup water
1/4 tsp. thyme
3/4 tsp. ground ginger
1 head cauliflower
1 head lettuce
1 large onion, chopped
1 lb. bacon, cooked
and crumbled
1-1/2 cups mayonnaise
1/2 cup Parmesan cheese
1/4 cup sugar

Cook bacon until crisp; crumble and set aside. Brown chicken in bacon grease and drain. Return crumbled bacon to pan. Add onions, mushrooms and green beans, if you like them.

In a bowl, combine cranberry sauce, water, soup mix, thyme and ginger. Pour over chicken and simmer for 40 minutes. Good with potatoes, or pour over rice.

Betty Higgins
Presque Isle, ME

Seafood Casserole

1/2 cup margarine
1 green bell pepper, chopped
2 cups mushrooms
4 celery stalks
4 cloves garlic, minced
1 lb. scallops
4 oz. cooked crab meat
6 oz. cooked shrimp
2 10-1/2-oz. cans cream
soup (your choice)
2 cups milk
2 cups instant white rice
breadcrumbs

Sauté pepper, mushrooms, celery and margarine until tender. Stir in scallops, crab and shrimp until hot. Remove from heat. Prepare rice as directed on package. Stir into seafood mixture. Stir in cream soup and milk. Spoon mixture into 2-1/2 quart casserole. Sprinkle breadcrumbs on top. Bake at 350° for 45 minutes to 1 hour. Enjoy!

Geraldine Tufts
Norridgewack, ME

Spiedi Marinade

1/2 leg of lamb
(venison, beef or pork)
1-1/2 cups red wine vinegar
1/2 cup combined oil
(10% olive oil and
90% vegetable oil)
2 tsp. dried basil leaves
3 garlic cloves, halved
1 tsp. dried rosemary
1 tsp. bay leaf
1 tsp. dried parsley flakes
1/2 tsp. lemon juice
1/4 tsp. dried oregano
1/4 tsp. dried thyme
1/8 tsp. cayenne
pepper (optional)
black pepper to taste
(fresh ground)
salt to taste

Trim and cut meat into 1" cubes. Mix remaining ingredients in glass bowl or sealable bag, and add meat. Marinate for 3 - 5 days, stirring thoroughly each day. Skewer meat onto spiedi sticks or kabob sticks — not too tightly — leaving 3 - 4" space at each end. Grill, turning once, until meat is done. Remove meat from sticks, keeping warm. Place 5-6 cubes in a slice of Italian bread. Now, all you need to enjoy the meal is a good salad.

Lois Hart
Johnson City, NY

Spiedi Marinade

• •

Pick Me Up Festive Casserole

1 large yam
1 16-oz. bag frozen peas
and carrots
1 16-oz. canned yam
1 can condensed celery soup
1 5-oz. bag croutons
1/2 can French's onion rings

In 3 quart casserole dish, mix celery soup and 2/3 can water until smooth. Add all ingredients to casserole dish and mix gently. Top with onion rings. Microwave for 8 minutes. Be sure to pierce yam before microwaving. Serve.

Joan Zim
Swoyerville, PA

No Tomato Pasta

1 onion, diced
1 garlic clove, minced
olive oil
1 T. butter, melted
1/2 tsp. dried parsley
1/4 tsp. dried oregano
pinch ground black pepper
angel hair pasta

Cook onion and garlic in olive oil until tender. Mix butter, parsley, oregano and ground pepper. Combine all ingredients in a bowl with cooked angel hair pasta. Mix well.

Maureen Goodwin
Framingham, MA

Enchilada Pie

1 1/2 lbs. hamburger
1 medium onion, chopped
8 fresh green chiles, seeded
    and chopped
1 clove garlic, minced
salt
pepper
1 pkg. enchilada sauce mix
1/4 cup picante sauce
10-inch flour tortillas
olives (optional)
10 oz. Cheddar cheese, shredded
10 oz. Monterey jack
    cheese, shredded

In a skillet, cook hamburger, onion, green chiles, garlic, salt and pepper until hamburger is browned. Set aside. Prepare enchilada sauce and mix according to package directions. Add picante sauce. In a pie pan, layer 1/3 sauce mixture, flour tortillas, 1/2 meat mixture, 1/2 of the cheeses, tortillas, 1/3 sauce mixture, meat mixture, tortillas, remainder of sauce, and then remainder of cheeses. Top with sliced black olives, if desired. Bake at 300° for 20-30 minutes (or microwave on high for 5-10 minutes).

Darlene Brown
Coalgate, OK

Runza's

1 lb. hamburger
1/2 head cabbage
2 carrots, grated
1 medium onion, chopped
dry oregano
salt
pepper
hot sauce
2 loaves frozen bread
    dough, thawed
grated cheddar cheese

Brown hamburger. Set aside. Sauté cabbage, carrots, onion, oregano, salt, pepper and hot sauce until vegetables are tender. Mix vegetables with browned hamburger. Slice each loaf of dough into 4 pieces. Flour a plate, and lay a slice of dough on the plate and flatten. Place a spoonful of mixture (1/8 of it) into the center of the dough and add small amount of cheese. Pull up the edges of bread dough and seal. Bake at 375° for approximately 20 minutes, or until golden brown.

Kelly A. Workman
Clearwater, FL

Gyoza

2 lbs. ground pork
1/2 head cabbage
1/2 head Chinese cabbage
(Bok Choy)
2 medium onions
1 carrot
3-5 green onions
3-5 cloves garlic
salt
pepper
2 pkgs. Gyoza (wonton)
skins/wraps
canola oil

Sauce:

2/3 cup white vinegar
1/3 cup soy sauce

Place pork in large bowl. Finely chop all vegetables. Add vegetables to pork. Thoroughly mix by hand. Add salt and pepper to taste. Fill each gyoza wrap by placing a teaspoonful of the pork mixture in the center of the skin. Spread a little water or egg yolk along the outer edge of the skin with your finger, fold over skin, and press to seal it. Place the gyoza on a baking sheet. Heat a 1/4" layer of oil on medium heat in a fry pan. When oil is hot, lay gyozas in pan and fry until golden brown on both sides. Serve with sauce mixture and white rice.

Nancy Case
Chalfont, Pennsylvania

Kielbasa

2 lbs. coarsely ground pork butt
1 lb. finely ground beef
1-1/2 tsp. coarse salt
1-1/2 tsp. crushed peppercorns
1-1/2 tsp. dried marjoram
1 T. paprika
2 cloves garlic, minced
sausage casings (optional)

Thoroughly mix the ingredients (with the exception of the casings) together. Shape into patties or stuff into casings. Refrigerate for 2-3 days to allow the flavors to blend. Fry the patties until golden brown, or simmer the links in water for 30 minutes. Kielbasa may be frozen for 1-2 months.

Linda Safran
St. Marys, PA

Vegetable Meat Pie

1 lb. ground beef
1 cup soft breadcrumbs
1 8-oz. can seasoned
tomato sauce
1 egg
1 tsp. salt
1 tsp. chili powder
dash cayenne pepper
10 oz. frozen mixed vegetables
1 tsp. garlic salt
1/2 cup grated sharp
cheddar cheese

Heat oven to 350°. Combine ground beef, breadcrumbs, 1/3 cup of tomato sauce, egg, salt, chili powder and cayenne. Press mixture into 9-inch pie plate, building up the edges. Bake for 10 minutes.

While meat shell is baking, season mixed vegetables with garlic salt. Fill meat shell with vegetables and pour remaining tomato sauce over top. Bake for 25 minutes, or until vegetables are tender. Sprinkle grated cheese over top and bake for 5 more minutes.

Charlotte Ott
Farmington, MI

Cabbage Rolls

1-1/2 cups cooked rice
12 large cabbage leaves
1 lb. ground beef
1 lb. ground pork
1 8-oz. can tomato sauce
1 medium onion, chopped
1 medium bell pepper, chopped
2 tsp. salt
1/2 tsp. cayenne pepper
1/8 tsp. black pepper
1/8 tsp. garlic powder
1 8-oz. can vegetable juice

Combine meats, cooked rice, onion, bell pepper, tomato sauce and seasonings. Dip cabbage leaves in boiling water for 4 minutes. Drain. Place 1/12 of rice/meat mixture in each cabbage leaf and roll up. Place rolls in pan seam-side-down and cover with juice. Bake at 350° for 1-1 1/2 hours. Baste often.

Lisa Lejeune
Kaplan, LA

Main Dishes

Breast of Chicken Maria

4 skinless, boneless
chicken breasts
salt
pepper
all-purpose flour
3 T. butter or vegetable oil
12 fresh asparagus spears

Sauce:

1 cup chicken broth
3 T. dry sherry (optional)
1/2 tsp. lemon juice
1/8 tsp. minced garlic
1/4 cup butter
2 T. all-purpose flour
3/4 cup shredded
provolone cheese
1 cup sliced fresh mushrooms
1/2 cup lump crab meat
1/4 tsp. cracked black pepper

Season chicken breasts with salt and pepper; dredge in flour to coat. Sauté in butter until golden brown and cooked through. Steam asparagus until tender.

While chicken breasts and asparagus are cooking, prepare sauce by bringing chicken broth to a boil in a saucepan and adding sherry, lemon juice, and garlic. In a separate pan, melt 1/4 cup butter and stir in 2 tablespoons flour. Add this to simmering broth mixture, stirring constantly until sauce thickens. Reduce heat to low. Add cheese, mushrooms, crabmeat and pepper. Cook 2-3 minutes over low heat, stirring constantly.

Place sautéed chicken breasts on serving platter. Top each with 3 asparagus spears and ladle crab meat sauce over each serving.

Susan Stitch
Florissant, MO

Greek Eggplant

1 cup dried tomatoes
1 cup hot water
1/4 cup butter
2 onions, sliced
1 16-oz. can tomato sauce
1 15-oz. can pitted black
olives, drained
1 large eggplant
1 T. ground cinnamon

Soak dried tomatoes in the hot water for 1 hour. Melt butter in large kettle and sauté onions. Add tomato sauce and black olives. Cut soaked dried tomatoes into small pieces with scissors and add to kettle. Allow this mixture to simmer.

Cut eggplant into 1/2" cubes. Add eggplant and cinnamon to the sauce. Simmer 30 minutes, or until eggplant is tender, stirring frequently and adding water if necessary. Consistency should be like stew and will thicken as it simmers. May be served over rice.

Janet Morehouse
Owing Mills, MD

Spaghetti Sauce

1 lb. hamburger
2 8-oz. cans tomato sauce
1 15-oz. can tomatoes
1 small onion, chopped
3 T. brown sugar
1 tsp. Worcestershire sauce
1 tsp. dried parsley flakes
1/2 tsp. garlic salt
1/2 tsp. dried basil leaves
1/2 tsp. chili powder
1/2 cup ketchup
1/2 tsp. ground oregano

Combine all ingredients in a saucepan. Simmer over medium heat for an hour or two, stirring as needed.

Elmyra Wolf
Arapahoe, NE

Tamale Pie

1 pkg. corn bread mix
1 lb. hamburger
1 15-oz. can whole kernel corn,
    drained
1 15-oz. can tomato sauce
1 15-oz. can pitted black olives,
    drained
1 onion, chopped
1 bell pepper, chopped
1 hot pepper, chopped
1 T. chili powder
1 large clove garlic, minced
2 cups grated cheddar cheese

Prepare corn bread mix according to directions to make batter, but do not bake. Mix together hamburger, corn, tomato sauce, olives, onion, peppers, chili powder and garlic. Spread mixture in a 9 x 13-inch pan. Sprinkle 1 cup of grated cheese over mixture. Pour corn bread mixture over meat/cheese mixture. Sprinkle 1 cup of grated cheese on top. Bake at 350° for 1 hour.

Marjorie Crump
Holdenville, OK

Glazed Barbecue Ribs and Beans

4-5 lbs. pork ribs, cut into
serving pieces

Glaze:

1/2 cup chopped onion
1 T. vegetable oil
1 32-oz. bottle ketchup
1-1/3 cups brown sugar
2 T. Worcestershire sauce
2 bay leaves, halved
4 slices bacon, chopped
1 32-oz. can pork and beans
2 T. brown sugar
1 cup glaze

Bring a large pot of water to a boil. Add ribs, and simmer for 25 minutes. Meanwhile in a large saucepan, sauté onion in oil for 5 minutes. Add remaining glaze ingredients. Bring glaze to a boil. Reduce heat to low, simmer 30 minutes.

Fry bacon until crisp and set aside. Drain off 1/3 cup of liquid from pork & beans. Mix beans in saucepan with bacon, brown sugar and 1 cup of glaze. Simmer on low until ready to serve. Drain ribs, brush with glaze and grill about 25 minutes, brushing and turning every 5 minutes.

Ellen Schumer
Perryville, MO

Creamy Tomato Sauce

2 cloves garlic, minced
2 T. butter
6-8 large tomatoes, chopped
1/2 tsp. salt
1/4 tsp. freshly ground pepper
1/2 cup whipping cream
2 T. chopped fresh basil

In a saucepan, cook garlic in butter over medium heat for 1 minute. Add tomatoes, salt and pepper. Cook, uncovered, for 12-15 minutes, until thickened. Gradually stir in cream and basil. Cook over low heat for 10 more minutes. Serve over hot cooked vermicelli noodles.

Linette Graham
Naperville, IL

Irish-Italian Spaghetti

1 large onion, diced
1 medium green (or red)
bell pepper
2 cups sliced fresh mushrooms
2 T. butter
1 16-oz. can diced tomatoes
2 10-1/2-oz. cans tomato soup
2 10-1/2-oz. cans cream of
mushroom soup
salt
pepper
2 tsp. chili powder
1/4 tsp. hot pepper sauce

In a medium saucepan, sauté onion, bell pepper and mushrooms in butter until soft, 10-15 minutes. Add tomatoes, soups, chili powder, hot sauce and salt and pepper to taste. Add meat and simmer 2-4 hours, stirring occasionally. Serve over hot cooked pasta noodles.

Kevin Kinney
Racine, WI

Asparagus Casserole

2 cans tall asparagus
1/2 lb. Velveeta cheese
8 boiled eggs, sliced
1 small jar chopped pimento
1/2 stick butter
1/4 cup flour
1 cup milk
pepper

Drain asparagus juice from cans. Pour juice into stew pan. Stir constantly until thickened. Add pimento, milk, salt and pepper. Put one can's worth of asparagus across bottom of casserole pan. Top asparagus with 4 slices of boiled egg, half of the cheese, half of the sauce mixture. Repeat for second layer. Top with buttered crumbs. Bake until lightly browned.

Wilma Jensen
Lufkin, TX

Knedlike Zeli Bohemian Style

8 medium potatoes, peeled
4 cups all-purpose flour
2 eggs, beaten
4-5 lbs. spare ribs
1 medium onion, sliced
1 large can sauerkraut

Cook and mash potatoes. Let cool. Combine potatoes, flour and eggs on a floured board. Separate into four balls. Roll out into long strips. Cut into bite-size pieces. Cook dough pieces 20 minutes in boiling, salted water. Do not overcook.

Cook spare ribs in roasting pan. Pour off excess grease. Add onion and sauerkraut. Cook at 375° until all ingredients have melded, approximately 30 minutes. Add dumplings to meat and sauerkraut. Serve hot or cold.

Ann Whitehill
Blair, NE

Harvest Moon Supper

1-1/2 lbs. lean ground beef
1 cup oatmeal
3/4 cup evaporated milk
1/4 cup chopped onion
1/4 cup ketchup
1-1/2 tsp. salt
1/4 tsp. black pepper

peaches:

1 15-oz. can peach halves
brown sugar
white vinegar
whole cloves

sauce:

1 10-1/2-oz. can cream
of mushroom soup
1 tsp. Worcestershire sauce
2/3 cup evaporated milk

Combine meat mixture ingredients. Shape into six patties and place in shallow pan. Bake at 350° for 20 minutes.

Place a pinch of brown sugar in centers of peach halves, then fill with vinegar. Place whole cloves around middle. Add to pan with patties and bake for another 15 minutes.

Combine soup and Worchestshire sauce in a saucepan. Heat over medium heat. Gradually stir in evaporated milk and heat until steaming, but not boiling. Serve sauce over patties with peaches.

Tracy Callow
Stevensville, MD

Chicken Burrito

4 boneless, skinless
chicken breasts, cubed
1 bunch fresh cilantro, chopped
1 medium onion, chopped
2 15-oz. cans diced
Mexican tomatoes
2 T. ground cumin
salt
pepper
1 package flour tortillas
1 cup shredded sharp
cheddar cheese
1 cup sour cream
1 avocado, peeled and mashed
picante sauce

Place chicken, cilantro and onion in a large, ungreased skillet. Cook over medium heat until chicken is done. Add tomatoes, cumin, salt and pepper. Cook until mixture is thickened. Warm tortillas as directed on package. Fill tortillas with meat mixture, cheese, sour cream, avocado and picante sauce. Roll up tortillas, enclosing filling.

Janie Robinette
Henley, MO

Pizza Lasagna

1 16-oz. pkg. uncooked
lasagna noodles
2 15-oz. cans pizza sauce
2 8-oz. pkgs. mozzarella cheese
1 can large olives (sliced)
2 cans sliced mushrooms
1 pkg. pepperoni
parmesan cheese to taste

Boil lasagna noodles in large pan until tender. Drain.

Preheat oven to 375°.

Grease lasagna pan. Spread a layer of sauce on bottom. Layer lasagna noodles on top of sauce. Spread sauce on top of noodles. Add a thin layer of olives and mushrooms. Sprinkle lightly with parmesan cheese. Layer with pepperoni. Sprinkle mozzarella cheese on top. Lay lasagna noodles on top of cheese. Repeat until you have made enough layers to reach the top of the pan, ending with the mozzarella cheese on top.

Bake until the cheese on top turns golden brown.

Cool for about 15 minutes before cutting and serving.

Luana Haverty
Mineral Wells, WV

Ratatouille

4 onions, sliced
2 cloves garlic, minced
1/4 cup olive or cooking oil
4 tomatoes, seeded and chopped
1-1/2 tsp. dry thyme
1 tsp. salt
1 bay leaf
1/4 tsp. pepper
1 large eggplant
6 medium zucchini, cut
    into strips
3 large green peppers, cut
    into strips
6 large mushrooms
parmesan cheese

Cook onions and garlic with oil in Dutch oven until tender. Add undrained tomatoes and seasonings. Simmer 10 minutes.

Discard bay leaf. Remove and set aside 2 cups of sauce mixture.

Slice eggplant in half lengthwise and then cross-wise into 1/2" slices. Arrange half of eggplant, half of zucchini, half of peppers and half of mushrooms over sauce in Dutch oven. Sprinkle with salt and pepper. Cover with 1 cup of reserved sauce. Arrange remaining vegetables on top and sprinkle with salt and pepper. Pour remaining 1 cup sauce over and cover.

Simmer 20 minutes, uncover and simmer 15 minutes more. Serve hot with parmesan cheese sprinkled on top. (You can also bake this at 350° for 1 hour.)

Jane Seymour Cartwright
Crawford, CO

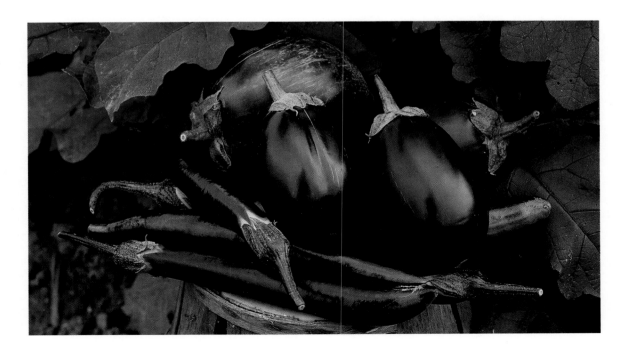

CHAPTER 6

Relishes

Ripe Tomato Relish

9 lbs. tomatoes, peeled
and cut up
7 onions, finely chopped
1 lb. celery, finely chopped
1/2 cup pickling salt
6 cups sugar
2 red and green bell
peppers, finely chopped
2 cups white vinegar
4 tsp. mustard seeds

Mix the tomatoes, onions, celery and salt in glass or plastic container. Let sit for 2-4 hours. Drain in a colander or jelly bag. Discard the salty juice. Add the remaining ingredients and mix well. Put in plastic or glass jars, but do not press to seal. Keeps in refrigerator indefinitely.

Janet Stewart
Maxwell, IA

Ripe Tomato Relish

Pickled Beets

beets
2 cups sugar
2 cups white vinegar
1 lemon, thinly sliced
1 T. cinnamon
1 T. cloves
1 tsp. allspice

Scrub the beets extra clean before cooking so you can save 2 cups of the beet water for the recipe. Cook the beets in enough water to cover them, over medium heat until tender, then cool and peel off the skins. Slice or quarter beets. Combine 2 cups beet water and the remaining ingredients in saucepan. Cook over medium heat to dissolve sugar and form a syrup. Add the beets to syrup and simmer for 15 minutes. Pack in jars and seal.

HINT: A little grated fresh horseradish added to beets gives a great variation.

Rita K. R. Hussey
Columbia, MO

Pickled Beets

Easy Salsa

2 green bell peppers, chopped
2 hot yellow peppers, seeded
and chopped
2 jalapeño peppers (more if you
want it hotter), seeded
and chopped
1 large onion, chopped
1/2 bunch fresh cilantro,
chopped
2 tsp. dried minced garlic (or 3
cloves fresh garlic, minced)
4 qts. diced, canned tomatoes,
drained with juice reserved
4 cups water
1 6-oz. can tomato paste
1 8-oz. can tomato sauce
1/4 cup white vinegar
1/2 cup white sugar
2 tsp. salt
1 tsp. dried oregano
1 tsp. dried basil

Put peppers, onion, cilantro and garlic into a large pot. Add the water and the reserved tomato juice. Bring to a boil and boil for about 15 minutes, or until the vegetables are slightly tender. Add the diced tomatoes and the remaining ingredients; return to a boil. Boil for 5 minutes. Put salsa into quart jars with 2-part lids and process in a hot water bath for 15 minutes.

Sharon Skrivseth
Moyie Springs, ID

Homemade Root Beer

2 cups cane sugar
2 T. root beer extract
1/2 tsp. powdered baker's yeast

Take a clean 2-liter plastic soft drink bottle and pour the sugar into it with a dry funnel. Swirl the sugar in the bottom of the bottle to make a well to catch the extract. Carefully pour in the extract. Fill the bottle half way with water and swirl to dissolve the ingredients. Add the yeast and swirl again. Fill the bottle to within 2 inches from the top. Screw the cap on tightly to seal. Leave the bottle at room temperature until the bottle feels hard (about 4 days). Place in the refrigerator overnight and serve.

HINT: There will be some bitter sediment on the bottom of the bottle. Pour off the root beer to avoid this. Substitute other extracts to change the flavor of the beverage.

Mark Tobler
Erlanger, KY

Punch Slush

6 cups water
4 cups sugar
4 cups pineapple juice
2 1/2 cups orange juice
3 medium bananas, smashed
1/2 cup lemon juice
lemon-lime soda

Mix all ingredients, except soda, stirring until sugar is dissolved. Place mixture in freezer until slushy. Fill cups with slush and cover with lemon-lime soda.

Joann Herrera
Magna, VT

Pickled Green Tomatoes

1 clove fresh garlic, whole
2 tsp. salt
1/2 tsp. sugar
green tomatoes, washed
and halved or quartered
water
white vinegar

Put the garlic, salt, sugar and tomatoes into a quart canning jar with a 2-part lid. Boil 3 parts water to 1 part vinegar to form a brine. Pour the brine over the tomatoes in the jar, put lid on and process for 15 minutes in a hot water bath.

HINT: Double, triple, etc. the recipe to make as many quarts as you want.

Makes 1 quart.

Irene Brown
Garfield, NJ

Pickled Green Tomatoes

3 green or red peppers, sliced
2 hot peppers (can use more),
whole or sliced
5 large onions, sliced
2-6 qts. kettle green tomatoes,
cut into quarters
salt
2 cups sugar
2 cups white vinegar
celery seed to taste
mustard seed to taste

Salt the peppers, onions and tomatoes overnight in 1/4 cup salt per kettle. Drain the next day. Bring the sugar and vinegar to a boil with the celery seed and mustard seed. Add the peppers, onions and tomatoes. Boil for just a few minutes until tender. Put in jars and seal.

Jeanette Schwartz
Crivitz, WI

Pickles

6 cucumbers
2 small sprigs of dill
2 cloves garlic
2 peppercorns
2 cloves
1 bay leaf
1 gallon hot water
1 cup white vinegar
1/4 cup salt

Wash and dry the cucumbers. Put 1 sprig of dill, 1 clove garlic, 1 peppercorn, 1 clove and 1 bay leaf into the bottom a big jar. Then add the cucumbers. Now put the remaining dill, garlic, peppercorn and clove on top of the cucumbers.

In a bowl, mix the water, vinegar and salt to make a brine. Cover the cucumbers with the brine. Let the cucumbers soak in the brine in the refrigerator. After a few days a foam will appear at the top of the brine. Be sure to remove the foam every day. The pickles will be ready in 2-4 weeks.

Scott Johnson
Columbus, OH

Pickles

Strawberry or Raspberry Punch

2 cups orange juice
2 cups strawberries
or raspberries
1 cup water
2 cups lemonade
1/2 cup sugar
2 liters ginger ale
(or lemon-lime soda)
ice cubes

Put strawberries or raspberries in a punch bowl. Stir in the sugar, and let stand for 1/2 hour. Add the orange juice, lemonade and water, mixing well. Just before you are ready to serve the punch, add the ginger ale or soda and the ice cubes.

Marian M. McNabb
Linn Grove, IA

Mama Hall's Green Tomato Ketchup

1 gallon green tomatoes
4-6 medium onions
4-6 tart red apples
4 bell peppers
jalapeño peppers (optional)
1/2 cup canning salt
3 cups white vinegar
2 cups sugar
1 cup water
1 T. pickling spice, tied
in a cloth

Chop the vegetables like you would to make a fine coleslaw. (I use my food processor.) Core apples but do not peel, the color looks pretty in the jars. In a bowl, combine vegetables and canning salt. Cover and let stand overnight.

The next day, drain off the liquid. In a stockpot, combine vegetables, vinegar, sugar, water and pickling spice. Bring to a boil and simmer for 30 minutes. If you wish to can the relish, pack in hot pint jars and process in boiling water for 5 minutes. Otherwise, just refrigerate. This keeps almost indefinitely.

Makes 6 pints.

Melody Rose
Benton, KY

Dilled Okra

3 lbs. okra
celery leaves
garlic cloves
dill sprigs
1 qt. water
2 cups white vinegar
1/2 cup salt

Pack the okra in hot jars with a few celery leaves, 1 clove of garlic and 1 sprig of dill per jar. Combine the water, vinegar and salt, and bring to a boil. Pour over the okra. Adjust the lids and process for 10 minutes in a boiling water bath. Let the okra stand for 3-4 weeks before using.

Makes 6 pints or 3 quarts.

Mozelle S. Woodring
Newton, NC

Dilled Okra

Dried Fruit Honey Oatmeal

3 1/2 cups water
1/2 cup chopped dried fruit
(apples, raisins, pears,
cranberries or apples)
2 cups quick or old-fashioned
oats, uncooked
1/3 cup honey
1/2 tsp. ground cinnamon
1/4 tsp. salt

In a 3-quart saucepan, bring the water and dry fruit to a boil. Stir in the oats and return to a boil. Reduce heat to medium and cook 1 minute for quick oats or 5 minutes for old-fashioned, or until most of the liquid in absorbed, stirring occasionally. Stir in the honey, cinnamon and salt and serve.

John Patuc
Munhall, PA

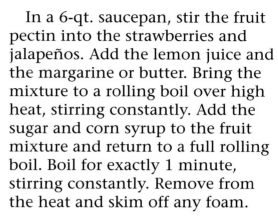

Strawberry-Jalapeño Sauce

*3-1/2 cups crushed strawberries
(fresh or frozen)
1 cup finely chopped jalapeño
peppers (about 9)
1 pkg. fruit pectin
3 T. lemon juice
1/2 tsp. margarine or butter
4 cups sugar
1 cup corn syrup*

In a 6-qt. saucepan, stir the fruit pectin into the strawberries and jalapeños. Add the lemon juice and the margarine or butter. Bring the mixture to a rolling boil over high heat, stirring constantly. Add the sugar and corn syrup to the fruit mixture and return to a full rolling boil. Boil for exactly 1 minute, stirring constantly. Remove from the heat and skim off any foam.

Immediately fill clean 8-oz. jars to within 1/8 inch of the tops. Wipe jar rims and threads if necessary. Cover quickly with flat lids, and screw bands on tightly. Invert the jars for 5 minutes then turn upright. Let them stand at room temperature for 24 hours. Unopened sauce may be stored in a cool, dark place for up to a year.

Makes approximately 4 pints of sauce.

HINT: This sauce can be used on cream cheese and served with crackers as an appetizer, as a marinade for chicken, or even as an out-of-the-ordinary ice cream topping.

Kory Hagler
Bismarck, ND

Brandy Slush

2 cups boiling water
2 bags green tea
7 cups water
2 cups sugar
1 12-oz. can frozen orange
juice concentrate, thawed
1 12-oz. can frozen lemonade
concentrate, thawed
2 cups brandy
lemon-lime soda or ginger ale

Use 2 cups of boiling water to brew the tea. Set aside. Bring the 7 cups of water to a boil and stir in the sugar. Combine the tea, orange juice, lemonade, brandy and sugar-water. Pour into a sturdy, freezer-proof container and freeze. Frozen consistency will be mushy.

When ready to serve, place an ice cream scoop portion (or two) into a glass. Add lemon-lime soda or ginger ale. Stir and serve.

Marilyn J. Banzhaf
Whitefish Bay, WI

Mother's Corn Relish

13 cups fresh or frozen corn
11 cups chopped cabbage
3 red or green bell peppers
1-1/2 cups sugar
2 cups white vinegar
2 T. salt
2 T. celery seed
2 T. mustard seed
2 T. vegetable oil or olive oil

Mix all of the ingredients together, except for the oil. Bring to a boil. Boil for about 10 minutes. Remove from heat and stir in the oil. Pack, boiling hot, into sterile jars and seal at once.

Louise G. Ybright
Chester, ID

Marinade For Beef

1/4 cup soy sauce
2 T. vegetable oil
2 T. red wine vinegar
2 T. honey
1 tsp. ground ginger
1 clove garlic, crushed

Mix all ingredients together and use to marinate beef overnight.

Veronica M. Guarraia
Somerville, NJ

Accident Barbecue Sauce

2 cups ketchup
2 cups cider vinegar
1 cup water
3/4 cup dark brown sugar
1/4 cup black molasses
1/4 cup Worcestershire sauce
1 T. black pepper (optional)
1 T. red pepper (optional)
1/4 tsp. celery seed (optional)
dried parsley flakes, to taste
onion powder, to taste
garlic powder, to taste
2 drops liquid smoke (optional)

Mix all ingredients together in a large pot and bring to a boil. Reduce the heat and simmer for 30 minutes. Keeps up to 2 months in the refrigerator.

Makes 2 quarts.

Dawn M. Vanthorn
Columbia, NC

Tomato Gravy

2 slices bacon, diced
1 medium onion, diced
3-4 ripe tomatoes, peeled
and quartered

Brown bacon over medium heat. When the bacon is nice and crisp, add the onion and cook until it is translucent. Add the tomatoes and cook until the desired consistency has been achieved.

Serve over hot cooked rice, baked potatoes or hot biscuits.

HINT: I use a small iron skillet, the tomatoes draw iron into the gravy.

Beverly Tindell
Hartford, AL

Refrigerator Pickles

4-5 cucumbers,
washed and sliced
3 cups sugar
3 cups white vinegar
1/3 cup coarse salt
1-1/2 tsp. tumeric
1 tsp. celery salt
1 tsp. mustard seeds

Combine all ingredients in glass container. Let it sit in the refrigerator for a week. Then they are ready to eat.

Coriena Richmond
Chesaning, MI

Salsa

16 cups chopped tomatoes
4 cups chopped onions
2-1/2 cups white vinegar
2 cups chopped green bell
peppers
1 cup sugar
1/2 cup chopped jalapeño
peppers (can use more or less to
taste)
1/3 cup salt
1-1/2 T. chili powder
2 tsp. ground cumin
2 tsp. pepper
1 tsp. alum

Combine all ingredients in large pot. Bring to a boil. Reduce heat, and simmer for 1 1/2 hours. Put into jars and seal.

Makes 4 quarts.

Barb Jansen
Bertha, MN

Pickling Cucumbers or Green Tomatoes

*hard pickling cucumbers
or green tomatoes
pickling spice
garlic cloves, thinly
sliced
(fresh dill sprigs)
celery (for green tomatoes)
coarse salt
rye bread*

Wash the cucumbers or green tomatoes and pack them in layers in clean gallon jars. To each layer add 1 T. pickling spice, 1 clove garlic and a few sprigs of dill. For tomatoes, add a few pieces of celery. Fully pack jars.

Make a brine by dissolving coarse salt in cold water, to suit taste. Pour brine over cucumbers or tomatoes to cover them completely. Next, place a piece of rye bread wrapped in cheesecloth in the top of the jar. Cover the of the jar with a piece of cheesecloth and secure with a cord of string.

For well-done pickles, allow 2 weeks for fermentation. For half-done pickles, about 4 days. Tomatoes take a full 2 weeks. When pickles are done, remove the cheese-cloth and the bread. Cover the jars tightly and store in a cool place until needed.

Sidney H. Hersh
Silver Spring, MD

Stove-Top Apple Butter

6-7 lbs. cooking apples,
unpeeled, cored and quartered
3 cups water
1 tsp. ground cinnamon
1 stick cinnamon
(about 4 inches long)

In a 6-8-qt. heavy kettle, bring the apples and water to a boil, reduce the heat, and simmer until the apples are tender. Press the cooked apples through a colander or food mill. Discard the peels. Return the apples to the kettle and add the remaining ingredients. Simmer, uncovered, stirring frequently, until the consistency is very thick and the color is dark brown, about 8 hours. Remove cinnamon stick. Freeze in containers or process in jars as for jam.

Makes 4-6 cups.

Anna Farmer
Hot Springs, AR

CHAPTER 7

Side Dishes

Cider Roasted Squash

*8 cups peeled and seeded winter
squash, cut into 1-inch cubes
1 medium onion, cut into wedges
1/4 cup apple juice or cider
2 T. olive or cooking oil
1 T. brown sugar
1/2 tsp. salt
1/4 tsp. pepper
1/4 tsp. ground nutmeg or ginger*

In a greased 3 qt. rectangular baking dish, combine the squash and the onion. Combine the juice or cider, oil, brown sugar, salt, pepper and spice and pour over the vegetables. Bake uncovered in a 450° oven for about 35 minutes or until tender, stirring twice.

Makes 8 servings.

HINT: Some winter squashes are easier to peel than others. For acorn and other ridged squash, bake with the peel on and then remove it after cooking.

Rita Miller
Lincolnwood, IL

Cider Roasted Squash

Kiss Me Kate, Cauliflower

1 head cauliflower
1 cup white flour
1 egg
1 cup milk
salt
shortening or vegetable oil

Heat about 1/2-inch of shortening or vegetable oil in a large skillet. Break the cauliflower into medium-size pieces. Beat the egg into the milk to make a dipping mixture. Dip the fresh cauliflower into the dipping mixture, then roll in flour to coat.

Place the cauliflower pieces in the skillet and cook slowly over medium heat, turning often, until the cauliflower turns a golden brown and a fork slides easily through them. Remove the pieces from the skillet and drain on paper towels. Salt to taste.

Makes approximately 3 polite servings.

Kathleen R. Couture
Waurika, OK

Zucchini Boats

4 medium zucchini
16 oz. sour cream
shredded colby or cheddar cheese

Boil or steam the zucchini until fork-tender. Cut the zucchini lengthwise and remove the pulp. Fill the empty zucchini halves with sour cream up to the edges and sprinkle the tops with cheese. Put the boats under the broiler until the cheese is melted and bubbly.

Judy Ward
Centereach, NY

Tex-Mex Hominy

6 slices bacon, chopped
1 onion, halved and sliced
1 can white hominy, drained
1 can yellow hominy, drained
1 tsp. chili powder
1/4 tsp. garlic powder
1/2 bell pepper, diced
salt

In a skillet, sauté the bacon and onions until the bacon is cooked. Add the bell pepper, the hominy and the spices (except the salt). Cover, and cook on medium heat for 15 minutes. Salt to taste and serve.

Gail Moore
Dime Box, TX

Tex-Mex Hominy

Parmesan Carrot Bake

1 cup packed grated carrots
1 cup mayonnaise
1 cup parmesan cheese

Mix the ingredients together in a oven-proof bowl and bake at 350° for 35 minutes, or until you can't stand the aroma any longer. Serve hot on wheat crackers.

Chris Peurifoy
Menifee Valley, CA

Fried Green Tomatoes

3/4 cup self-rising flour
1/4 cup cornmeal
1/4 tsp. salt
1/4 tsp. pepper
3/4 cup milk
3 green tomatoes, cut into
1/4-inch slices
vegetable oil

Combine the flour, cornmeal, salt, pepper and milk and mix until smooth. Add more milk to thin, if necessary; the batter should resemble pancake batter. Working in batches, dip the tomato slices into the batter and allow the excess to drip off. Fry in 2 inches of hot oil (375°), in a large skillet, until browned, turning once carefully with tongs. Transfer to paper towels to drain.

Yields 3 servings.

Laura White
Paramus, NJ

Fried Green Tomatoes

Debbie's Delight

3-4 medium potatoes
1/2 onion, diced
1/2 cup hazel nut or vanilla
coffee creamer or half-and-half
1/4 tsp. tarragon
3 T. water
salt
pepper

Thinly slice the potatoes and place in a lightly oiled fry pan with the onions. Cook on medium until the onions are translucent and the potatoes are browned. Add the water and cover. When half of the water is reduced, add the creamer and tarragon. Cover and reduce until the liquid is creamy. Salt and pepper to taste.

Debbie L. Reis
Alpharetta, GA

Grilled Zucchini Rounds

1-1/2 tsp. lemon juice
4 T. olive oil
1 T. minced onion
1 T. soy sauce
1-1/2 tsp. dill weed
1/8 tsp. garlic powder
1/8 tsp. pepper
pinch salt
4 6-8-inch zucchini
grated parmesan cheese

Combine all of the ingredients, except for the zucchini and parmesan, to form a marinade. Cut the zucchini every inch to make rounds. Pour the marinade over the zucchini and let it sit for 2-3 hours.

Skewer the zucchini on shish-ka-bob skewers. Place the skewers on the grill covered with tin foil. Turn them over when partially done and sprinkle with parmesan cheese. Cook to a tender bite and serve.

Pat Skewes
Marshall, MN

Broccoli Noodle Side Dish

8 oz. uncooked wide noodles
3-4 cloves garlic, minced
1/4 cup olive or vegetable oil
4 cups broccoli florets
1/2 lb. fresh mushrooms, thinly
sliced
1/2 tsp. dried thyme
1/4 tsp. pepper
1 tsp. salt (optional)

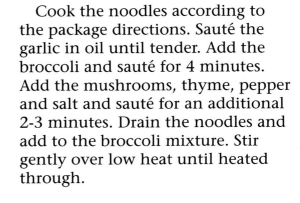

Cook the noodles according to the package directions. Sauté the garlic in oil until tender. Add the broccoli and sauté for 4 minutes. Add the mushrooms, thyme, pepper and salt and sauté for an additional 2-3 minutes. Drain the noodles and add to the broccoli mixture. Stir gently over low heat until heated through.

Yields 8 servings.

Virginia Williams
Oklahoma City, OK

Picnic Potatoes

5 lbs. potatoes
1 onion, chopped
2 slices bread, diced
1/2 cup milk
1 green pepper, chopped
3/4 lb. processed soft
cheese, cubed
1/2 lb. margarine or
butter, melted
crushed corn flakes

Boil the potatoes with the skins on, then peel and cube. Mix in the onion and pepper. Add the cheese and bread cubes. Pour the melted butter or margarine and the milk over the potato mixture and stir thoroughly. Pour into a lightly greased baking pan and sprinkle with the crushed corn flakes until well coated. Bake for 1 hour at 350°.

Christine Summers
Levittown, PA

Onions Au Gratin

2 large onions
1 chicken bouillon cube
3/4 cup boiling water
1/4 tsp. thyme
1 T. butter
salt
pepper
1/2 cup bread crumbs
2 T. melted butter
1/2 cup grated sharp
cheddar cheese

Cut the onions into slices and arrange them in a pan, overlapping slightly. Dissolve the bouillon cube in the boiling water. Add the thyme and then pour over the onions. Dot with butter and sprinkle with salt and pepper. Cover and bake for 20 minutes at 400˚.

Toss the bread crumbs in the melted butter. Add the cheese to the onion mixture. Sprinkle the buttered bread crumbs over the onions and bake uncovered for another 10 minutes, or until the crumbs are crisp and golden.

Makes 5 servings.

Michelle Post
Minersville, PA

Grilled Corn on the Cob

fresh corn
cold water
foil

Use as many ears of corn and you have room for on the grill. Pull back, but do not remove, the husks from the corn. Remove as much silk as you can (the rest will come off easily after cooking). Pull the husks back up over the kernels.

Place the corn in a pan of cold water and soak for at least 20 minutes. Remove the corn from the water and wrap each ear in foil (with the husks still on). Place on the grill or directly over the hot coals and cook for about 10 minutes on each side. Remove the foil and husks (be careful the corn will be very hot). Serve immediately.

HINT: An easy way to butter the corn is to butter a piece of soft bread and then rub the bread across the corn. It makes the bread taste great too.

Patricia Larkins
Homewood, IL

My Favorite Potato Pancakes

2 eggs
1/2 small onion
1 tsp. salt
2 T. flour
1/4 tsp. baking powder
2 cups cubed raw potatoes
oil for frying

Put the eggs, onion, salt, flour, baking powder and 1/2 cup cubed potatoes into a blender and blend. When the mixture is smooth, add the remaining potatoes and blend. Pour the pancakes into a greased frying pan and cook.

Iris Hiltbrunner
De Forest, WI

Skillet Squash

1/4 cup butter
4 cups thinly sliced squash
1 onion, sliced
1 tsp. salt
pepper to taste
2 tomatoes, sliced
1/2 cup grated cheddar cheese

Melt the butter in a large skillet. Add all of the other ingredients, except for the cheese, and cook, covered, until tender. Be careful not to overcook. Sprinkle with the cheese and heat until it is melted.

Makes 4-6 servings.

Suzanne Guleke
Amarillo, TX

Yellow Squash Casserole

1 lb. yellow squash, cut up
1 onion, chopped
1 tsp. salt
1/2 stick butter, melted
1 heaping T. sour cream
1 egg
1 can French fried onion rings, divided
1/2 cup grated cheddar cheese
1/2 roll crackers, crushed
1/2 stick butter, melted

Cook the squash and the onion in a small amount of water until tender. Drain and mash well. To the squash and onion mixture, add the salt, 1/2 stick melted butter, sour cream, egg, 1/2 cup French fried onion rings, and the cheddar cheese. Pour into a greased baking dish and bake in a 375° oven for 30 minutes.

Remove the dish from the oven top with 1/2 can onion rings, cracker crumbs and 1/2 stick melted butter. Return to the oven and cook until brown.

Serves 6.

Betty Dunlap
Montgomery, AL

Corn Pudding

1 can cream corn
1 can whole kernel corn
1 stick margarine, melted
4 T. flour
1 cup sugar
1 tsp. salt
2 tsp. vanilla
3 eggs, beaten
1 cup milk

Combine the sugar and the flour and add it to the remaining ingredients, mixing well. Pour into a casserole dish and bake for 1 hour at 325°.

Geneva (Billie) Hensley
Sandston, VA

Stuffed Artichokes

Seasoned Bread Crumbs:

9 cups fine bread crumbs
3 cups grated romano cheese
1 tsp. salt
2 tsp. pepper
1 cup parsley flakes
2 tsp. garlic salt or 2 cloves
garlic, finely minced
and 1 tsp. salt

Artichokes:

4 medium artichokes
1 cup oil, olive or vegetable
2 eggs, lightly beaten
with a little water
2-3 cloves garlic
1 tsp. oil, olive or vegetable
salt

Put all of the seasoned bread crumb ingredients into a bowl and mix well. Cut the tips of the leaves and a small portion of the tops off of the artichokes. Even out the bottoms so the artichokes will stand. Wash them and drain them upside down.

Slowly mix the oil into the crumbs so that they lightly stick together (you may need more or less than 1 cup). Open the centers and the leaves gently and stuff the artichokes with the crumb mix. Set them in a large pot and pour the egg mixture gently over the crumbs to seal them.

Add water half way up the artichokes and drop in the cloves of garlic, about 1 tsp. of oil and a dash of salt. Cover the pot and bring the water to a boil, then simmer for about 1 hour until the leaves are tender and the centers are cooked.

HINT: Serve these as a side dish or as a meal. Eat the tender parts of the leaves, the crumbs and the heart, but do not eat the center (the choke) as it contains needles that give the artichoke its name.

Madeline A. Parisi
Fair Haven, MI

Baked Onions and Apples

4 mild onions, sliced
4 apples, peeled, cored and sliced
2 T. brown sugar
1/4 cup butter
salt
pepper

In a greased 2-qt. casserole, layer the onions and apples, ending with a layer of apples. Sprinkle with brown sugar and dot with small bits of butter. Bake at 350° for 1 hour.

Serves 6.

Marilyn Carr
Lauderdale-By-The-Sea, FL

Baked Onions and Apples

Cheese and Zest Banana Peppers

20-24 fresh ripe banana peppers
10-12 slices American cheese
2 T. margarine
lemon pepper

Preheat the grill. Wash the peppers and pat dry. Remove the stems and follow by making a slit almost the full length of the peppers. Place 1/2 slice of cheese on each pepper and arrange in the center of heavy duty foil. Add the margarine to the top of the peppers and season to taste with lemon pepper. Wrap the foil around the peppers well and poke several holes in the top. Cook on the grill for 30-40 minutes.

Alice J. Day
Oklahoma City, OK

Country Green Beans with Sesame Seeds

2 cups fresh green beans
1-2 rounded tsp. sesame seeds
2 tsp. sugar
1 tsp. ginger
1/2 tsp. dry mustard
water

In a large, non-stick frying pan, place the green beans and enough water to well cover the bottom of the pan. Mix in the sugar, mustard, ginger and sesame seeds. Simmer over medium-low heat until the beans are tender.

Sharon Walker
Huntington Station, NY

Squash Cakes

1-1/4 cups coarsely
grated summer squash
1/4 cup chopped onion
10 soda crackers, crushed
4 eggs
oil for frying
salt

Mix all of the ingredients together, adding enough egg to bind the ingredients together. Spoon into a hot, lightly oiled skillet and flatten to make 4" cakes. Fry to a golden brown on each side. Salt before turning, if desired.

David E. Williams
New London, IA

Vegetarian Rice

1 sweet red pepper, finely chopped
2 celery stalks, finely chopped
1 large onion, finely chopped
1 large or 2 medium carrots,
finely chopped
2-4 cloves roasted garlic
1 T. extra virgin olive oil
salt
pepper
1 cup peas, fresh or frozen
2/3 cup uncooked long grain rice
1-2/3 cups vegetable
stock (homemade is best)
1 chili pepper, chopped
and diced (optional)

Sauté the red pepper, celery, onion, carrots and garlic in the oil for 2-3 minutes. Do not brown. Add the salt and pepper to taste, peas, rice and stock. Add the chili pepper if desired. Cover and simmer for 20 minutes after bringing it to a boil.

Janet Marson
Newark, VT

Southern Greens

1-2 bunches greens (turnips, mustards or collards)
2-4 cups chicken stock
1 medium onion, chopped finely
pork of choice (pork chops, neck bones, bacon, ham hock, etc.)
salt
pepper
1-2 tsp. sugar

Wash the greens well and chop them coarsely. Place the greens into a pot with the chicken stock (chicken stock should fill half the pot). Add the onion and the pork and bring to a brisk boil. Reduce the heat to simmer and cook, covered, until tender. The greens will cook down and you may add more chicken stock if desired. Add the salt and pepper to taste and the sugar to remove any bitter taste.

Carol C. Lowery
Eastman, GA

CHAPTER 8

Desserts

Summer Blackberry Crisp

1/2 cup blackberries,
   fresh or frozen
2 cups rolled oats
1/2 cup oat bran
1/2 cup unbleached white flour
1/2 cup brown sugar
1/3 cup canola or safflower oil

Preheat the oven to 350°. In a large baking dish (9 x 13 inch), which has been lightly greased, place the berries. In a medium size bowl, combine the remaining ingredients and mix. Spread the topping evenly over the berries. Bake for 35-45 minutes, until the berries are bubbly and the topping is crisp. Allow to cool before serving.

HINT: This may be served warm or cold and is delicious with vanilla ice cream on the side.

Holly Hockstadt
Seattle, WA

Summer Blackberry Crisp

Summertime Fruit Trifle

1 box pound cake mix
1/3 cup sugar
1/4 cup all-purpose flour
1-1/2 cups milk
1 egg
1 T. butter
1 tsp. finely shredded orange peel
1/2 cup orange juice
2 T. cream sherry or orange juice
2 cups peeled peach slices,
fresh or frozen
2 cups sliced strawberries
1/2 cup blueberries,
fresh or frozen
1 cup reduced-fat frozen
non-dairy topping

Prepare a pound cake according to the directions on the box, but bake in a 8 x 8 x 2 inch baking pan. Set aside.

To make a custard sauce: In a heavy medium size sauce pan, combine the sugar and flour. Stir in the milk and eggs and cook, stirring, over medium heat until the mixture is thick and bubbly. Cook and stir for 1 minute more then remove from the heat. Stir in the orange peel and 1/2 cup orange juice. Cool thoroughly.

To assemble the trifle: Cut the cake into 1 1/2" cubes. In a 2 qt. glass bowl, arrange half of the cake cubes. Sprinkle them with half of the sherry or orange juice. Top with half of the fruit. Pour half of the custard over the fruit and then repeat all of the layers. Pipe or spread the non-dairy topping on the top. Cover and chill until it is time to serve. If desired, you can garnish with additional fruit and mint.

Makes 10 servings.

Flo Grumm
Ridge, NY

Lemon Cake

Cake:
1 package lemon gelatin
1 package lemon cake mix
4 eggs
3/4 cup hot water
3/4 cup oil
juice of 1/2 lemon
Lemon Icing:
1 cup powdered sugar
3 T. lemon juice

Mix the gelatin and the hot water together and set aside to cool. Mix all of the rest of the cake ingredients together and then add the gelatin. Bake at 350° until done. Mix the icing ingredients together and spread on the cake while it is still hot.

Adrella Hester
Westville, OK

Apple Brown Betty

2-1/2 cups graham
cracker crumbs
1/2 cup melted butter
or margarine
6-8 apples, peeled and sliced
3/4 cup brown sugar
3/4 cup hot water
1-1/2 tsp. cinnamon
1/2 tsp. nutmeg
2 T. lemon juice
raisins (optional)
walnuts or pecans (optional)

Grease a pan and preheat the oven to 350°. Pour the lemon juice over the sliced apples. Place the apples in the greased pan. Combine the graham cracker crumbs, melted butter, brown sugar and spices. Pour this mixture over the apples and add the raisins and nuts if desired. Pour the hot water over the apples and crumb mixture. Dot with butter. Bake at 350°, covered, for 1 hour.

Lisa Zucatti
Hazleton, PA

Peanut Butter Cookies

1/2 cup peanut butter
1/2 cup brown sugar
1/2 cup white sugar
1/4 cup butter or margarine
1 egg
1 tsp. baking soda
1 cup flour

Cream the butter, sugar and peanut butter. Add the egg and then the flour and baking soda. Roll 1/2 teaspoon dough in hand to form a small ball. Place on a pan and press with a fork. Bake at 400° for no longer than 15 minutes.

Nellie Webb
Athens, TN

Homemade Ice Cream with Chocolate Sauce

Ice Cream:
3 cups milk
1-1/2 cups sugar
4 eggs, beaten well
1 qt. half-and-half
1 pt. whipping cream
3 T. vanilla
Chocolate Sauce:
1 square unsweetened chocolate
1 cup cold water
1 cup sugar

To make the ice cream: Combine the milk and the sugar in a heavy saucepan and bring to a boil. Add the eggs slowly to the hot mixture, stirring well. Turn the heat down and simmer, uncovered, until the mixture has a custardy consistency. This takes about 45 minutes to 1 hour. Cool completely. When you are ready to freeze the ice cream, put it in a gallon freezer container and add the half-and-half, the whipping cream and the vanilla. Freeze according to your ice cream freezer's directions.

To make the chocolate sauce: Put the unsweetened chocolate and the water in a saucepan and bring to a boil. Add the sugar and stir well. Bring to a boil again then remove from heat.

Linda Butler
Underwood, WA

Apple Crunch Caramel Sauce

Apple Crunch:
5 cups pared and sliced apples
(about 5 medium)
1/2 tsp. cinnamon
1/4 tsp. nutmeg
1-1/2 cups biscuit baking mix
1/2 cup milk
1/8 tsp. cinnamon
Caramel Sauce:
1/4 cup biscuit baking mix
1 cup brown sugar (packed)
1/2 tsp. salt
1 tsp. vinegar
1 cup water
1 tsp. vanilla
1 T. butter or margarine

To prepare the caramel sauce: Blend the baking mix, sugar and salt in a saucepan. Stir in the water and vinegar. Cook, stirring constantly, over medium heat until the mixture thickens and boils. Boil and stir 1 minute and then remove from heat. Stir in vanilla and butter. Allow the sauce to cool.

To make the apple crunch: Heat the oven to 400°. Place the apples in an ungreased 8 x 8 x 2 inch pan and sprinkle with the 1/2 tsp. cinnamon and the nutmeg. Stir the baking mix and the milk to a soft dough. Spread or drop the dough over the apples and sprinkle with the 1/8 teaspoon cinnamon. Pour the caramel sauce over the top. Bake for 35 minutes or until the apples are tender.

Serves 6.

HINT: Yellow delicious apples work well.

Domer and Carolyn Wiltrout
Scottdale, PA

Chocolate Chip Cheesecake

1-1/2 cups graham
cracker crumbs
1/3 cup cocoa
1/3 cup sugar
1/3 cup butter or
margarine, melted
3 8-oz. pkgs. cream
cheese, softened
1 14-oz. can low-fat, sweetened
condensed milk
3 medium eggs,
at room temperature
2 tsp. vanilla extract
1 cup mini chocolate
chips, divided
1 tsp. all-purpose flour

Heat the oven to 300°. In a bowl, combine the graham cracker crumbs, cocoa, sugar and butter. Press this mixture evenly onto the bottom of a springform pan. In a large mixer bowl, beat the cream cheese until it is fluffy. Gradually add the milk, beating until smooth. Add the eggs and vanilla and mix well.

In a small bowl, toss half of the mini chips with the flour to coat and then stir into the cheese mixture. Pour into a prepared pan and sprinkle the remaining chips over the top. Bake for 1 hour. Turn the oven off and allow the cheesecake to cool in the oven for 1 hour. Remove from the oven and cool to room temperature. Refrigerate.

Tammy Fleming
Russellville, AR

Regina Cookies

1 stick margarine or 1/2 cup
shortening
1 cup sugar
3 eggs
1 tsp. vanilla
2-1/2 cups flour
1/4 tsp. salt
1 T. baking powder
milk
sesame seeds

Mix the margarine, sugar, eggs and vanilla. Add the flour, salt and baking powder. Chill the dough and then roll into small balls and dip in milk and then sesame seeds. Bake at 375° for 8-10 minutes.

Evelyn Krzeszinski
Conway, AR

Strawberry Glaze Short Pie

1 qt. strawberries
1 cup water
1 cup sugar
3 T. cornstarch
1 baked pie crust

Wash, drain, hull and slice the strawberries. For the glaze: simmer 1 cup of berries with 2/3 cup water for 3 minutes. Blend the sugar, cornstarch and remaining water and stir into the hot mixture. Boil for 1 minute, stirring constantly. Color if you wish. Cool and then pour the remaining strawberries into a baked crust and cover with the glaze. Refrigerate until firm.

HINT: Top with whipped cream or ice cream.

Carolyn Skarke
Daury, TX

Scotcheroos

1 cup sugar
1 cup corn syrup
1 cup peanut butter
6 cups crispy rice cereal
6 oz. chocolate chips
6 oz. butterscotch chips

Combine the sugar and the corn syrup in a 3-qt. saucepan and cook over medium heat, stirring frequently, until the mixture begins to bubble. Remove from the heat and add the peanut butter, mixing well. Add the rice cereal and stir until well blended. Press into a buttered 9 x 13-inch pan. Melt the chips and spread over the cereal mixture. Cool and then cut into bars.

Margaret Tack
Hillsboro, OR

Janet's Blueberry Pie

*1 small container non-dairy
whipped topping
8 oz. sour cream
1/2 cup sugar
1/3 cup boysenberry syrup
fresh blueberries
1 graham cracker pie crust*

Mix the whipped topping, sour cream, sugar and syrup until well blended. Take enough blueberries to fill the crust heaping full and add them carefully so they don't get smooshed. Pour into prepared crust and refrigerate until cool and firm.

HINT: You may also put shaved chocolate and drizzled boysenberry syrup on top of the pie before serving.

Janet Marie Blaisdell
Newport, NH

Fruit Pizza

Crust:
1/2 cup soft butter
3/4 cup powdered sugar
1/2 tsp. lemon flavoring
1 tsp. vanilla flavoring
1 egg
1 tsp. cream of tartar
1 tsp. baking soda
1 1/4 cups flour
Topping:
8 oz. cream cheese
1/3 cup powdered sugar
fresh fruit, cut up
Glaze:
1/2 cup sugar
1/2 cup water
2 tsp. cornstarch
2 T. dry apricot gelatin
1 T. lemon juice

To make the crust: Mix all of the crust ingredients together and roll out on a pizza pan. Bake at 350° until it is light brown. Cool.

For the topping: Combine the cream cheese and powdered sugar and spread on the cool crust. Top with any cut-up fresh fruit that you want (bananas, kiwis, peaches, etc.).

To make the glaze: Cook the sugar, water and cornstarch until it is thickened. Add the dry apricot gelatin and the lemon juice. Drizzle over the fruit and chill.

Kathy McKittrick
Tobaccoville, NC

Aunt Jane's Date Nut Cookies

1 cup granulated sugar
2-1/2 cups chopped dates
1 cup water
1 cup black walnuts
1 cup margarine
2 cups brown sugar
3 eggs
1/2 tsp. baking soda
1/2 tsp. salt
4 cups flour

Combine the granulated sugar, dates and water and simmer for 30 minutes until mushy. Cool. Cream the margarine, brown sugar and eggs until fluffy. Add the baking soda, salt and flour. Divide into 4 equal parts. Roll 1/4" thick and spread with the date mixture. Roll on waxed paper and chill overnight. Slice the rolls into 1/4" pieces and bake at 375° for 10 minutes.

Makes 5 dozen cookies.

Bonnie Griffith
Hagerstown, MD

Applesauce Cake

2 eggs
2 cups sugar
1 tsp. baking soda, dissolved in a little water
2 cups applesauce
4 T. margarine, softened
2 tsp. cinnamon
1 tsp. cloves
1 tsp. ginger
1 tsp. nutmeg
3/4 cup raisins
1 cup walnuts
3 cups flour

Mix all of the ingredients together. Grease and flour a pan (bundt pans work well). Bake for 1 1/2 hours at 350°.

HINT: Glaze the cake and decorate it with candy orange slices.

Linda Sanders
Lawrensville, IL

Chocolate Layer Torte

1 8-oz. pkg. cream cheese
2 small pkgs. instant
  chocolate pudding
2 8-oz. cartons non-dairy
  whipped topping
1 box graham crackers
1/2 cup powdered sugar
3 cups milk

Lay down a layer of graham crackers on the bottom of the pan, cut to size for edges. Mix the cream cheese with one carton of the whipped topping and the powdered sugar and then spread the mixture over the layer of crackers. If the cream cheese is softened in the microwave first, and the whipped topping is thawed, they spread much better.

Lay down another layer of crackers. Putting aside 2 tablespoons of the pudding mix, mix the milk with the rest of the two packages of pudding mix. Spread this mixture over the crackers.

Lay another layer of crackers over the pudding. Mix the remaining 2 tablespoons of pudding mix with the last carton of whipped topping and spread over the last layer of crackers. Refrigerate for 6 hours to pull everything together.

Tamera Pritzl
Sturgeon Bay, WI

Fruit Basket Cake

1 box white cake mix
1/3 cup melted butter
3 eggs
1-1/3 cups water
2 bananas, 1 mashed
and 1 sliced
2 cups sweet dried cherries
blueberries, strawberries,
blackberries or raspberries
additional berries for garnish
whipped cream or non-dairy
whipped topping

Preheat the oven to 350°. Grease and flour a tube pan. Place the cake mix in a bowl and add the butter, eggs, water and mashed banana. Mix until well blended. Add the berries and cherries. Bake for 40-45 minutes until done. Let the cake cool.

Split the cake through the middle and place the sliced bananas and whipped cream between the layers. Place the top over the bottom and cover the top with whipped cream and garnish with dried berries and cherries.

HINT: If you dry fruit from the summer months to use in this cake, it tastes great.

Jennifer Pierce
Citrus Heights, CA

Custard Pumpkin Pie

6 eggs yolks
3/4 cup brown sugar
3/4 cup granulated sugar
2 cups fresh pumpkin
1/2 cup cornstarch
1/4 tsp. salt
1/4 stick butter
1 tsp. pumpkin pie spice
1 tsp. vanilla
1 can evaporated milk
water
2 baked pie shells

Mix the dry ingredients together. Whip the egg yolks and then add the dry ingredients. Mix the milk with enough water to make 3 cups. Stir the milk mixture and the remaining ingredients into the rest and cook in a double boiler to thicken. Pour into baked pie shells.

Makes 2 pies.

Reta L. Smith
Beckley, WV

Orange Sponge Cake

Cake:
3 eggs, whites and yolks separated
1 cup sugar
1/3 cup orange juice
grated rind from 1 orange (2 T. reserved for the icing)
1 cup cake flour, sifted
1 tsp. baking powder
1/4 tsp. salt

Orange Icing:
1-1/2 cups granulated sugar
2 egg whites
6 T. orange juice
2 T. grated orange rind
1/4 tsp. cream of tartar

To make the cake: Put the egg yolks and whites into separate bowls. Beat the egg whites until stiff and add the egg yolks one at a time. Gradually add the sugar, then the orange juice, grated orange rind, flour, baking powder and salt. Bake in a square or small angel cake pan in a 350° oven for 35-40 minutes.

To make the icing: Mix the ingredients in the order given. Beat over hot water until the icing will hold up in stiff peaks. Cut the cake into layers and spread the icing between the layers, over the top and on the sides.

Lani Walker
Fitchburg, MA

Rich's Whiskey Cake

1 18-1/2-oz. box golden yellow
or French vanilla cake mix
2 5-3/4-oz. boxes instant
vanilla pudding
1-1/2 tsp. ground allspice
1 tsp. nutmeg
6 oz. applesauce
6 oz. orange juice
8 oz. bourbon or sour mash
whiskey (not blended)
4 large eggs
1/4 cup chopped pecans
1/4 cup walnuts
(English walnuts or hickory nuts)
2 oz. apricot Brandy
2 oz. peach Schnapps
2 oz. pear, apple or cherry
Schnapps

Mix the cake mix, pudding mix, allspice and nutmeg together with a spoon. Add the applesauce, orange juice and bourbon or whiskey. Mix for 2 minutes and then blend in the eggs and nuts. Mix well on high for 2 minutes. Fold into a greased 12-cup bundt pan. Bake at 325° for 35-40 minutes, until golden brown. Remove from the oven and let it cool in the pan for 15 minutes.

Mix together the apricot Brandy and the Schnapps. Baste the top and around the sides of the cake, and put back in the oven for 20 minutes or until done to a medium brown. Cool and place on a plate. Cover with plastic wrap or seal in a large plastic bag. Let the cake age for at least 3 days (more for better flavor). This will keep refrigerated for 2 months or more.

HINT: The alcohol content bakes off when the temperature is above 185° for 20 minutes or more, but the full flavor remains.

Richard Everhart
Clarksville, IN

Lemon Cream Pie

3 large lemons
1/3 cup cornstarch
1-1/4 cups sugar, divided
3 large eggs
1 pt. whipping cream
baked deep dish pie shell

Grate 2-3 tablespoons of lemon peel into long strips and set aside. In the top of a double boiler, mix the cornstarch and 1 cup sugar. Squeeze 1-1/3 cups lemon juice from the lemons and mix into the cornstarch and sugar mixture. At this point, you can add 1 tablespoon of the grated lemon peel, if desired. Cook and stir until very thick and clear. Remove from the heat.

In a small bowl, beat the eggs. Mix a little of the hot mixture into the eggs and then pour the eggs into the hot mixture. Cook for 3 minutes or until the mixture comes to a boil. Remove from the heat and cool completely, stirring occasionally.

Beat 1 cup whipping cream to stiff peaks and fold into the cooled mixture. Pour into the baked pie shell. Beat the remaining cup of whipping cream with 1/4 cup sugar. Top the pie with the whipped cream and garnish with the lemon peel.

Jeannie Edwards
Lewiston, ID

Red Raspberry Pie

Pie filling:
1-1/2 cups sugar
3 T. quick-cooking tapioca
dash salt
3 cups fresh red raspberries
1 tsp. lemon juice
1 T. butter or margarine
Pastry crust:
2 cups all-purpose flour, sifted
2/3 cup shortening
1 tsp. salt
5-7 T. cold water
butter
granulated sugar

To make the crust: Sift together the flour and salt. Cut in the shortening. Add and mix 1 tablespoon of water at a time until moistened. Divide the dough in half. Flatten on a lightly floured surface. Roll 1/8"-thick. Repeat with the other half of the dough.

For the filling: Combine the sugar, tapioca and dash of salt. Mix in the raspberries and the lemon juice. Let this mixture stand for 20 minutes. Put one of the rolled out pastry crusts into a 9-inch pie pan. Pour the raspberry mixture in and dot with butter. Adjust the top crust, trimming and fluting the edges. Cut slits in the top and sprinkle lightly with granulated sugar. Bake at 400° for 50 minutes.

Kimberly Steward
Marshalltown, IA

Pecan Cake Roll

4 eggs, separated
1 cup confectioners sugar
2 cups ground pecans
1 cup whipping cream
3 T. sugar
2 tsp. baking cocoa
1/2 tsp. vanilla extract
chocolate shavings and
additional confectioners
sugar

In a mixing bowl, beat the egg yolks and the confectioners sugar until thick, about 5 minutes. In another bowl, beat whites until soft peaks form, then fold into yolk mixture. Fold in pecans until well blended (the batter will be thin).

Grease a 15 x 10 x 1 inch baking pan lined with waxed paper and spread the batter in it. Bake at 375° for 10-15 minutes or until the cake springs back when touched lightly. Turn onto a linen towel that has been dusted with confectioners sugar. Peel off the waxed paper and roll the cake in the towel, starting with the short end. Cool on a wire rack for 1 hour.

While the cake is cooling, beat the cream, sugar, cocoa and vanilla in a mixing bowl until peaks form. Carefully unroll the cake and spread the filling over the cake. Roll up again and refrigerate. If desired, garnish with chocolate shavings and confectioners sugar.

Yields 10-12 servings.

Helen K. Shannon
Tunnelton, WV

Great Grandma Jeffer's Peanut Butter Fudge

2 cups confectioners sugar
1/2 cup milk
2 heaping T. peanut butter

Put all of the ingredients into a saucepan and cook over medium heat until it comes to a boil. Boil the mixture for exactly 5 minutes. Remove from the stove and stir until the mixture has thickened. Pour into a buttered pan. Cut in squares to serve.

Cindy Stidham
Aurora, CO

Pumpkin Bread

3 cups sugar
2 sticks margarine, melted
2 cups pumpkin
1 tsp. nutmeg
2 tsp. baking soda
1 cup nuts
4 eggs
2/3 cup water
1 tsp. vanilla
1 tsp. cinnamon
3-1/2 cups sifted flour

Mix all of the ingredients together and fill 4 greased 1-lb. coffee cans half full. Bake at 350° for 1 hour. This bread can be stored in the coffee cans.

Dotty Sellers
Harrisburg, PA

Pecan Chocolate Shortbread Bars

2 cups margarine, softened
3/4 cup granulated sugar
1 egg
2-3/4 cups flour
3/4 cup brown sugar
1/4 cup corn syrup
1 T. vanilla
3 cup chopped pecans
1 cup milk chocolate chips

Preheat the oven to 375˚. Spray a 15 x 10 inch pan with cooking spray and set aside. Beat 1 cup of margarine and the granulated sugar in a large bowl until the mixture is light and fluffy. Beat in the egg and vanilla. Slowly mix in the flour and beat until well mixed. Bake for 17 minutes. Remove from the oven.

While the dough is baking, mix the remaining margarine, brown sugar and corn syrup in a pan on the stove over medium heat. Stir continually until it comes to a boil. Stop stirring and let it boil for 3 minutes. Stir the pecans into the boiling mixture on the stove and then remove from the heat.

Pour the hot mixture over the dough and put it back in the oven for 18-22 minutes, or until it is bubbling. Remove from the oven and sprinkle the chips over the top, gently pressing them into the pecan topping. Let it cool for at least 30 minutes. Cut into bars.

Amy Agundez
Hayward, CA

Very Berry Cheesecake

*1-3/4 cups graham
cracker crumbs
1/4 cup sugar
1/3 cup melted butter
or margarine
3 8-oz. pkgs. cream
cheese, softened
1-1/3 cups (14-oz. can)
sweetened condensed milk
4 eggs
1/4 cup flour
2 T. lemon juice
1 8-oz. carton sour cream
fresh berries or fruit topping
of your choice*

Combine the graham cracker crumbs and sugar. Stir in the butter or margarine. Press onto the bottom of a 9 x 13 inch glass pan. Beat the cream cheese and the milk in a large mixer bowl. Beat in the eggs, flour and lemon juice. Pour into the crumb-lined pan. Bake in a moderate (350°) oven for 50 minutes. Spread with sour cream and bake an additional 10 minutes or until set. Cool and top with your favorite berries.

Diana Eoods
Boise, ID

Lemon Bisque

1 pkg. lemon gelatin
1 lemon, grated rind and juice
1-1/4 cups boiling water
4 T. sugar
1/8 tsp. salt
1 can evaporated milk, chilled
2 1/2 cups crushed
cookie crumbs

Mix all of the ingredients, except for the evaporated milk and the crumbs, together and cool (not hard set). With an electric beater, whip the can of milk until stiff. Fold the gelatin mix into the whipped milk. In a 8 x 12 inch glass baking dish, put part of the crushed cookie crumbs on the bottom. Spoon the gelatin mixture on top of the crumbs and spread. Sprinkle the rest of the crumbs on the top. Chill and cut into squares.

Elizabeth McDonald
Fort Edward, NY

Grand P'ere's

Sauce:
2 cups maple syrup
2 cups water

Dumpling dough:
2 cups flour
4 tsp. baking powder
1 tsp. salt
2 T. butter, softened
1 cup milk

To make the sauce: Mix the syrup and water together and bring to a boil. To make the dough: Combine the dry ingredients and then mix with milk and butter rapidly. Drop by the tablespoon into the boiling sauce. (Be careful not to splash yourself.) Cover and reduce the heat, simmering for 15 minutes. Serve warm with ice cream.

HINT: Do not lift the lid while dumplings are cooking as this will make them very tough.

Lori Pearce
Flint, MI

Red Beet Brownies

1/2 cup butter or
margarine, melted
1-1/2 cup sugar
2 eggs
1 tsp. vanilla
1-1/3 cups all-purpose flour
1 tsp. baking powder
1/2 tsp. salt
1 cup mashed or puréed red beets
1/3 cup beet juice
1 cup rolled oats
1/2 cup shredded coconut
1/2 cup chopped nuts

Preheat the oven to 350°. In a large bowl, combine the melted butter or margarine and sugar. Stir until well blended. Add all of the remaining ingredients, except for the nuts, and mix well until smooth. Pour the batter into two lightly greased 8 x 8 x 2 inch pans. Spread evenly and sprinkle with the nuts. Bake for 30 minutes.

James H. Dumas
Hope Valley, RI

Chocolate Zucchini Cake

1/2 cup soft butter
1/2 cup cooking oil
1-3/4 cups sugar
2 eggs
1 tsp. vanilla
1/2 cup sour milk
1 cup chocolate chips
2-1/2 cups flour
4 T. cocoa
1 tsp. baking soda
1/2 tsp. cloves
1/2 tsp. salt
1/2 tsp. cinnamon
2 cups grated zucchini
non-dairy whipped
topping (optional)

Cream the butter, oil and sugar. Add the eggs, vanilla and sour milk and blend. Add the flour, cocoa, baking soda, cloves, salt and cinnamon and stir together. Add the zucchini and 1/2 cup chocolate chips and mix well. Pour into a greased and floured 9 x 13 inch pan. Sprinkle with the remaining chocolate chips. Bake at 350° for 40 minutes. Cool and serve with whipped topping, if desired.

HINT: To sour the milk, add 1/2 tablespoon lemon juice to 1/2 cup milk and let it stand for about 5 minutes.

Connie Rebholz
New Berlin, WI

Devil's Food Cake for Angels

2-1/4 cups flour
1-1/2 cups sugar
3/4 cup shortening
2/3 cup cocoa
1-1/2 cups water
1-1/4 tsp. baking soda
1 tsp. salt
1 tsp. vanilla
1/2 tsp. baking powder
2 large eggs

Mix all of the ingredients together and beat on low for 30 seconds, then on high for 3 minutes. Bake in greased pans at 350° for 30-45 minutes. Check for doneness with a toothpick.

Yvette Sharp
Groves, TX

Toffee Crunch Cookies

40 salt crackers
2 sticks margarine
1 cup brown sugar
7 oz. chocolate chips
1 cup nuts (optional)

Line a cookie sheet with tin foil and place the crackers in a single layer. Melt the margarine, add the brown sugar and mix well. Pour over the crackers. Bake in a 350° oven for 8-10 minutes, until bubbly. Remove from the oven and sprinkle the chocolate chips over the top. When the chips have softened, spread them. Sprinkle with nuts, if desired. Remove from the pan before they begin to harden. If this happens, place back in the oven for a few minutes.

HINT: White chocolate is also excellent.

Caroline Aldrich
Woonsocket, RI

Zucchini Crisp

5 cups peeled and sliced zucchini
1 cup sugar
1 tsp. cinnamon
1/4 cup lemon juice
3/4 cup water
1 T. cornstarch

Topping:
1/3 cup soft butter
1/2 cup flour
1/2 cup brown sugar
1/2 cup oatmeal
3/4 tsp. cinnamon

Peel the zucchini and slice it lengthwise. Scoop out the seeds. Slice the zucchini to look like apple slices. Mix with the sugar, cinnamon, lemon juice and water and cook for 15 minutes. Mix the cornstarch in a small amount of cold water and add to the zucchini. Cook until thickened, stirring constantly. Pour into a greased 9 x 9 inch pan. Combine the topping ingredients and sprinkle on top of the zucchini mixture. Bake at 350° for 45 minutes.

Carol Rottman
Madras, OR

Ruby's Carrot Cake

2 cups flour
2 tsp. baking soda
2 tsp. cinnamon
1/4 tsp. salt
3 eggs
2 tsp. vanilla
3/4 cup canola oil
3/4 cup buttermilk
2 cups sugar
8 oz. crushed pineapple, drained
2 cups shredded carrots
3 1/2 oz. coconut
1 cup chopped nuts
(pecans or walnuts)

Beat the eggs, vanilla, oil, buttermilk and sugar together. Add the pineapple, carrots, coconut and nuts. Sift the dry ingredients together and add. Mix well. Bake in a well greased and floured 9 x 13 inch or bundt pan at 350° for 35-45 minutes. If you are using a bundt pan it takes longer. Cool and frost with an icing of cream cheese and powdered sugar.

Ruby Jewell
Aitkin, MN

Rich Chocolate Layer Cake

1/2 cup butter or margarine
2 tsp. apple cider vinegar
2 tsp. vanilla
2 cups warm water
3 cups all-purpose flour
2 cups sugar
6 T. cocoa powder
2 tsp. baking soda
1 tsp. salt

Melt the butter in a 1-qt. measuring cup in the microwave. Stir in the vinegar, vanilla and water. Set aside. Combine all of the dry ingredients in a large mixing bowl. Stir the butter mixture into the dry ingredients with a fork or medium whisk. Bake in two 8-inch prepared rounds, a lightly oiled coated 9 x 13 inch or 24 paper lined cup cake pans, at 350° for 35-40 minutes.

Anna L. Baker
Perryville, MD

Easy Apple Dumplings

1 package ready-made biscuits
4 apples, peeled and sliced into chunks half the size of a biscuit
2 cups sugar
2 cups water
cinnamon
1 stick margarine

Cut each biscuit in half and wrap the apples in the biscuits. Place in a 9 x 13-inch baking dish. Slice pats of margarine all over the tops of the dumplings and then sprinkle generously with cinnamon. Dissolve the sugar in the water and pour it over the dumplings. Bake at 350° for 30 minutes.

HINT: This is very good served with vanilla ice cream.

Jacque Dyson
Taylorsville, NC

Fabulous Carrot Cake

2 cups sugar
2 cups flour
2 tsp. baking soda
2 tsp. cinnamon
4 eggs, beaten
1 8-oz. can crushed pineapple
with juice
1-1/2 cups salad oil
2 tsp. vanilla
1 tsp. salt
1 cup flaked coconut
1 cup grated carrots
1 cup chopped pecans

Frosting:
6 oz. cream cheese, softened
1 cup powdered sugar
1/2 cup butter
1 tsp. lemon juice
dash salt

To make the cake: Sift the sugar, flour, baking soda and cinnamon. In a separate bowl, mix the eggs, crushed pineapple and juice, oil, vanilla, salt, coconut, carrots and pecans. Add the dry ingredients to the liquid mixture. Line three 8-inch cake pans with waxed paper. Pour the batter into the pans and bake at 350° for 35-40 minutes. Remove from the oven and allow to cool on cooling racks for 30 minutes.

Combine all of the frosting ingredients. When the cake is cool, frost the top of each layer and put together.

Kathy Spann
Mt. Pleasant, TX

Peach Bavarian Dessert

1 29-oz. can sliced peaches
2 pkgs. peach or apricot gelatin
(or a combination)
1/2 cup sugar
2 cups boiling water
1 T. almond extract
1 8-oz. carton whipping cream

Drain the peaches, reserving 2/3 cup juice. In a bowl, dissolve the sugar and gelatin in boiling water. Stir in the reserved peach juice and chill until slightly thickened. Chop the drained peaches in small pieces. Whip the cream until very stiff. Add the almond flavoring. Gently fold this into the gelatin mixture. Fold in the peaches. Pour into an oiled 6-cup mold and chill overnight. Garnish with more peaches or strawberries.

Bertha A. Mack
Gatlinburg, TN

Individual Apple Crisp

1 small apple, peeled and sliced
1 T. all-purpose flour
1 T. brown sugar
1 T. quick-cooking oats
1/8 tsp. cinnamon
dash ground nutmeg
dash salt
1 T. cold butter or margarine

Place the apple in a small greased baking dish. In a small bowl, combine the dry ingredients. Cut the butter in until crumbly. Sprinkle over the apple and bake, uncovered, at 375° for 30-35 minutes, or until the apple is tender.

Wilma Laurence
Toronto, KS

Dairy-Free Carrot Cake

3 cups flour
1/2 tsp. salt
1 tsp. baking powder
1 tsp. nutmeg
1 tsp. ginger
2 tsp. baking soda
3 tsp. cinnamon
1-1/2 cups safflower oil
1/2 cup lemon juice
2 cups frozen concentrated
apple juice
10-12 large carrots,
shredded or pureed
walnuts, pecans and
raisins to taste
all-fruit blueberry spread

Combine the flour, salt, baking powder, nutmeg, ginger, baking soda and cinnamon in one bowl. In a separate bowl, combine the oil, lemon juice and apple juice concentrate. Add the wet ingredients to the dry ingredients and mix well. Add the carrots, nuts and raisins. Fill two 9-inch cake pans with batter. Bake until a toothpick stuck in the middle comes out clean. When cooled, spread the blueberry spread over the top of one cake and layer with the second cake.

HINT: If you feel the recipe is not sweet enough for your taste, double the concentrated apple juice and reduce it by half before using.

Lisa Tarmu
Los Angeles, CA

Fig Cake

1 cup buttermilk
1 cup oil
3 eggs
1-1/2 cups flour
1 tsp. baking soda
1 tsp. salt
1 tsp. cinnamon
1 tsp. vanilla
1 tsp. allspice
1 cup nuts, chopped
1 cup fig preserves

Glaze:
1/2 cup buttermilk
1 cup sugar
3/4 stick butter
1/2 tsp. baking soda

Combine all of the cake ingredients and bake in a bundt pan at 375° for 1 hour. Combine the glaze ingredients and cook until the soft ball stage. Pour over the warm cake.

Elaine Romero
Kountze, TX

Overripe Fruit Bread

Fruit slush:
3 peaches, pitted
2 bananas, peeled
2 pears, cored
1/4 cup orange juice

Bread:
2 cups sugar
2/3 cup margarine, softened
4 eggs, slightly beaten
2/3 cup water
3-1/3 cups all-purpose flour
2 tsp. baking soda
1 tsp. salt
1/2 tsp. baking powder
1 T. cinnamon
1 cup nuts, coarsely
chopped (optional)
1/2 cup raisins (optional)

To make the fruit slush, blend the fruit and the juice together at high speed until smooth. This can be done either in a blender or food processor. Heat the oven to 350°. Spray two 9-inch loaf pans with a non-stick cooking spray.

Into a large bowl, sift together twice the flour, baking soda, salt, baking powder and cinnamon. Set aside. In a medium bowl, mix the sugar and margarine until creamy. Stir in the eggs until well blended. Beat in the fruit slush and water and continue to beat at medium speed for at least 1 minute. Pour the liquid ingredients into the large bowl containing the dry ingredients and fold together until moistened. Stir in the nuts and raisins, if desired.

Divide the batter between the two prepared pans. Sprinkle 2 teaspoons of sugar and cinnamon over the tops. Bake for 55-60 minutes, or until a toothpick inserted in the center comes out clean. Do not overbake. Remove from the oven and cool for 5 minutes. Remove from pans and cool completely on wire racks before slicing. Slice loaves into 12 slices each. Store in airtight containers to retain moisture.

HINT: This is a great way to use overripe fruit.

Debra A. Crain
Waynesville, MO

The Only Pumpkin Pie

*3 cups fresh pureed pumpkin
(peeled, diced and boiled)
2 cups granulated sugar
4 eggs
2 cans evaporated milk
3 tsp. cinnamon
1 tsp. nutmeg
1 tsp. ginger
1 tsp. allspice
1 tsp. ground cloves
1 tsp. salt
2 unbaked pie crusts*

Preheat the oven to 400˚. In a large mixing bowl, blend together the eggs and milk. Add the pumpkin, sugar, spices and salt. Pour into unbaked pie crusts. Bake pies for 1 hour. Cool completely.

Susan Perkins
Fulton, NY

Zucchini Brownies

2 cups flour
3 tsp. cocoa
1-1/4 cups granulated sugar
1-1/2 tsp. baking soda
1 cup walnuts
2 tsp. vanilla
1/2 cup corn oil
2 cups grated zucchini

Frosting:
2 cups powdered sugar
1/4 cup cocoa
1 tsp. vanilla
water

Mix the flour, cocoa, sugar, baking soda and walnuts together. Add the vanilla, oil and zucchini. Grease and flour a 9 x 13 inch pan. Spread the batter evenly (the batter will be very thick). Bake at 350° for 18-20 minutes.

To make the frosting: Combine the sugar, cocoa and vanilla. Add small amounts of water to this mixture until you get the desired consistency. Spread on the brownies.

John Marcucci
Kennard, NE

Zucchini Brownies

Rhubarb Custard Pie

2 cups sugar
1/4 cup flour
3/4 tsp. nutmeg
4 cups cut up rhubarb
3 eggs
3 T. milk
2 T. margarine
top and bottom pie crusts

Mix together the sugar, flour and nutmeg. Stir in the rhubarb. Beat the eggs and the milk together and stir into the rhubarb mixture. Pour into a pie crust and dot with margarine. Cover with a top crust, either lattice or with holes cut. Bake at 400° for 50-60 minutes.

Eileen Slinkman
Wisconsin Rapids, WI

Rhubarb Custard Pie

Tomato Spice Cake

2-1/2 cups fresh tomato puree
4 cups all-purpose flour
2-1/2 tsp. baking soda
1-1/2 tsp. salt
2-1/2 cups sugar
1/2 cup shortening
2-1/2 tsp. ground cinnamon
1 tsp. ground nutmeg
1 tsp. ground cloves
2 tsp. vanilla extract
1/2 cup chopped walnuts

Combine all of the ingredients, except for the walnuts, in a large mixing bowl. With an electric mixer, beat at low speed until well blended and then at high speed for 2 minutes. Pour the batter into a greased 10-inch tube pan, spreading evenly. Sprinkle with walnuts. Bake at 350° for 65 minutes, or until a wooden toothpick inserted in center of cake comes out clean. Cover with aluminum foil to prevent excessive browning, if necessary. Cool in pan on a wire rack for 10-15 minutes then remove the cake from the pan and let it cool completely on the wire rack.

Melodie MacDowell
Davidsonville, MD

Raspberry Fluff

4 cups fresh raspberries
(or 16 oz. frozen)
1/4 cup powdered sugar
1 envelope unflavored gelatin
2 T. cold water
1 pt. whipping cream

Crush the berries with the sugar. Soften the gelatin in the cold water and heat to dissolve. Stir into the berries. Fold in the whipped cream. Cover and refrigerate at least 4 hours. Spoon into dessert glasses.

LaVonne Robole
Inver Grove Heights, MN

Peanut Butter Cake

1 cup chunky peanut butter
2/3 cup butter or margarine
2 tsp. vanilla
2 cups brown sugar
4 eggs
1-1/2 cups flour
1 tsp. salt
4 tsp. baking powder

Mix all of the ingredients and bake for 20 minutes at 375°. Top with whipped cream before serving.

Sally Enders
Atlanta, GA

Maw Maw LaRues' Fruitcake

2 cups flour
2 cups milk
2 cups sugar
2 cups candied cherries
2 cups raisins
2 cups dried apples, cooked
1 cup pecan pieces and halves
1 cup walnut pieces and halves
1 capful orange flavoring
1 capful black walnut flavoring

Cook the apple slices over medium heat until tender. While the apples are cooking, begin mashing them until they have the consistency of applesauce. Put aside to cool. Combine the flour, sugar, milk and flavorings. Slowly add the applesauce mixture and then the other ingredients. Pour the mixture into a bundt pan and cook at 350° until done (usually 45-60 minutes). Cool and wrap in foil.

Donna LaRue
Blountsville, AL

Fruit Cocktail Cake

2 cups self-rising flour
1 tsp. baking soda
1-1/2 tsp. cinnamon
1 egg
1-1/2 cups sugar
sprinkle salt
1 tsp. vanilla
1 can fruit cocktail, with juice

Icing:
1 small can sweetened
condensed milk
1 cup sugar
1 stick butter or margarine
1 tsp. vanilla
1/2 cup nuts
1/2 cup coconut

Mix all of the cake ingredients together and pour into a long cake pan. Bake at 300° for 40 minutes. To make the icing: Bring the milk, sugar and butter to a boil and cook until it looks thick. Remove from the heat and add the vanilla, nuts and coconut. Pour over the cake while still hot.

Brenda Hermani
Londonville, OH

Mom Mom's Muscat Raisin Cake

1 box Muscat raisins
2-1/4 cups water
1 cup sugar
1/2 cup shortening
1 T. nutmeg
1 T. cinnamon
1 orange peel, finely chopped
1/4 cup coarsely
chopped walnuts
1 T. baking soda
1/4 cup warm water
2-1/2 cups flour
walnut halves
maraschino cherries

Mix the raisins, water, sugar and shortening together and bring to a boil. Boil for 15 minutes and then cool. Add the nutmeg, cinnamon, orange peel and walnuts. Mix the baking soda and warm water and then add to the mixture. Mix in the flour until blended. Pour into a greased and floured tube pan and decorate the top with the walnut halves and cherries. Bake for 30 minutes at 375°, then 30 more minutes at 350°.

Ed Pierzynski
Haddon Township, NJ

Rhubarb Dream Dessert

3 cups flour, divided
10 T. powdered sugar
1 cup butter or margarine
4 cups finely chopped rhubarb
2-1/4 cups sugar
3/4 tsp. salt

Blend 1 cup flour, powdered sugar and butter together and press into a 9 x 13-inch pan. Mix the remaining flour and other ingredients and pour over the crust. Bake at 350° for 40 minutes or longer, until the middle is set firm.

HINT: This can be used as a dessert or cut up into bars.

Janet Stewart
Maxwell, IA

Raspberry Chews

3/4 cup butter or margarine
3/4 cup white sugar
2 eggs, separated
1-1/2 cups white flour
1 cup chopped walnuts
1 cup raspberry preserves
1/2 cup flaked coconut

Cream the butter or margarine with 1/4 cup of the sugar until fluffy-light. Beat in the egg yolks. Stir in the flour until blended. Spread evenly in a 13 x 9 inch baking pan. Bake at 350° for 15 minutes or until golden brown. Remove from the oven.

While the bottom layer bakes, beat the egg whites until they are foamy and white and have doubled in volume. Beat in the remaining sugar until meringue stands in firm peaks. Fold in the walnuts. Spread the raspberry preserves over the layer in the pan and sprinkle with coconut. Spread the meringue over this.

Bake in a 350° oven for 25 minutes or until lightly brown. Cool completely and cut into squares.

Makes about 8 dozen bars.

Joanne M. Chandler
White Cloud, MI

Rhubarb Pie by Gramma Brickner

3 cups rhubarb, cut into
1-inch pieces
1 cup sugar
3 T. flour
butter
1 pre-cooked pie shell

Mix the rhubarb, sugar and flour together and put in the pie shell. Dot with butter and bake for 40-50 minutes at 400°.

Patricia Reiss
Wadsworth, OH

Vanilla Fruit Tart

Crust:

3/4 cup butter

1/2 cup confectioners sugar

1-1/2 cups flour

Filling:

1 10-oz. package vanilla milk chocolate chips

1/4 cup whipping cream

8 oz. cream cheese, softened

Fruit topping:

1/4 cup sugar

1 T. cornstarch

1/2 cup pineapple juice

1/2 tsp. lemon juice

assorted fresh fruit

Heat the oven to 300°. Beat the butter and sugar until they are light and fluffy, then blend in the flour. Press the mixture onto the bottom of a round pizza pan (up to 12-inch). Bake for 20-25 minutes, or until lightly browned. Cool completely.

To prepare the vanilla filling: In a microwave-safe bowl, microwave the chips and whipping cream on high for 1-1 1/2 minutes, or until the chips are melted and the mixture is smooth when stirred. Beat in the cream cheese. Spread this filling on the cooled crust. Cover and chill.

For the fruit topping: In a small saucepan, combine the sugar and cornstarch, then stir in the juices. Cook over medium heat, stirring constantly, until thickened. Remove from heat and cool.

Slice and arrange fruit on top of filling. Pour on the fruit topping and cover and chill.

Makes 10-12 portions.

Debbie Trautman
Cape Girardeau, MO

Vanilla Fruit Tart

Flavorageous Treats

5 T. margarine
1 16-oz. package miniature
marshmallows
1 small envelope unsweetened
drink mix (any flavor)
9 cups crispy rice cereal

Grease a 15 x 10 x 1-inch pan. Melt the margarine in 4-qt. saucepan on low heat. Add the marshmallows and stir until they are melted and the mixture is smooth. Remove from the heat and stir in the drink mix. Immediately add the cereal and mix until well coated. Spray a piece of wax paper with cooking spray to help you spread these treats evenly in the pan. Cool and cut with cookie cutters of your choice.

HINT: You can make these treats different colors and shapes for different occasions, red hearts, green shamrocks, orange pumpkins, etc.

S. Robinson
Mechanicsville, VA

Raw Apple Cake

2 cups sugar
1 cup melted butter
or margarine
4 cups chopped apples
1 cup brewed coffee
2 tsp. cinnamon
2 tsp. vanilla
2 tsp. baking soda
3 cups flour
brown sugar

Mix the butter, sugar, apples and coffee. Stir in the cinnamon, vanilla, baking soda and flour and mix well. Pour into a greased 9 x 13-inch oblong pan. Sprinkle the top with brown sugar. Bake at 350° for 40-45 minutes.

Rozella Eastman
Burkburnett, TX

Date-Filled Oatmeal Cookies

1 cup brown sugar
1 cup white sugar
2 cups butter or margarine
2 eggs
1/2 cup hot water
1 tsp. vanilla
4 cups flour
2 tsp. baking soda
1 tsp. salt
4 cups oatmeal

Filling:
1 cup raisins
1 cup chopped pitted dates
3/4 cup water
1-1/2 cups white sugar
1 T. white flour

Preheat the oven to 350°. Beat the margarine and sugar until creamy. Add the eggs, hot water and vanilla and beat well. Combine the flour, baking soda and salt and add to the margarine mixture, mixing well. Stir in the oats and mix well. Cover and chill for at least 1 hour.

To prepare the filling: Cover the raisins and dates with the water and simmer on low heat until tender, stirring constantly (about 15 minutes). Stir in the sugar and flour. Cool thoroughly.

Roll the dough 1/8- to 1/4" thick on a lightly floured board. Cut into circles and place on an ungreased baking sheet. Spoon 1 T. of filling on each cookie circle. Place a second circle on top and press the edges together. Bake for 10-12 minutes, or until golden brown. Cool completely.

Makes about 4 dozen cookies.

Joanne M. Chandler
White Cloud, MN

Strawberry and Banana Dessert

1 14-oz. can sweetened
condensed milk
1 cup cold water
1 small package nstant
vanilla pudding mix
1 pt. whipping cream,
stiffly whipped
1 pt. fresh strawberries,
cleaned, hulled and sliced
2 bananas, sliced and dipped
in lemon juice
1 10-12-oz. prepared butter
loaf or pound cake, cut into
12 slices
strawberry and banana slices
for garnish

In a large bowl, combine the milk and water. Add the pudding mix and beat well. Chill for 5 minutes. Fold in the whipping cream and then the strawberries and bananas. Line the sides and the bottom of a 3 1/2-qt. glass serving bowl with cake slices. Spoon the pudding mixture into the prepared bowl. Cover and chill. Garnish with strawberries and banana slices.

Judith Paquin
Woonsocket, RI

Mom's Oatmeal Cookies

1 cup shortening
1 cup brown sugar
1 cup white sugar
2 eggs
1-1/2 cups flour
1 tsp. salt
1 tsp. baking soda
3 cups rolled oats (regular are best, add some milk if the dough will not form clumps)
3/4 cup chopped walnuts

Mix the shortening, sugar and eggs. Mix the dry ingredients separately, then add to the wet, mixing thoroughly. Bake on greased cookie sheets for 10-15 minutes at 350°. (Bake one cookie sheet at a time on the center oven rack.) Allow the cookies to set for 30 seconds before removing them from the cookie sheet. The center of the cookies should be soft but not doughy.

Karen Burnett
Edinburg, PA

Gramma Brickner's Never Fail Pie Crust

4 cups flour
1-3/4 cups shortening
pinch salt
1 egg
1 T. vinegar
1/2 cup water
1 T. sugar

Mix the flour, shortening and salt together until crumbly. Make a hole in the center and add the remaining ingredients. Mix with a fork. Use lots of flour when rolling out.

This recipe makes enough dough for 3 pies.

HINT: I have tried cutting this recipe in half, but it doesn't come out as well as when you make a full batch. The dough, however, can be frozen up to 6 months for later use.

Patricia Reiss
Wadsworth, OH

Sally's Tofu Cheesecake

4 boxes firm tofu
1 cup honey
2 T. vanilla powder
4-6 tsp. fresh squeezed
lemon juice
Crust:
2 cups quick rolled oats
1 cup fine
unsweetened coconut
1/2 cup slivered almonds
dash salt
1 6-oz. can pineapple juice
Fruit jam:
1 package frozen
strawberries, thawed
6 oz. frozen apple juice
concentrate, hawed
3 heaping T. cornstarch

Mix all of the crust ingredients, except for the pineapple juice, right in a 13 x 9-inch pan. Add the juice to moisten the crust and stir in. Pat the crust level with a fork. Bake for 15 minutes at 350°, or until the crust is a golden brown.

Put the tofu, honey, vanilla powder and lemon juice in the blender and whiz until smooth. Pour into the pre-baked pie crust. Bring the berries and apple juice to a boil in a saucepan. Dissolve the cornstarch into it and cook until thickened. Cool before serving on your cheesecake.

HINT: Instead of the cornstarch, you can use 1/4 cup quick set powder. Just mix it into the fruit and juice. That way there is no cooking and more flavor.

Sally Hohnberger
Polebridge, MT

Banana Pudding

1 cup sugar, divided
3 T. self-rising flour
or 1-1/2 T. cornstarch
4 cups milk
1 tsp. pure vanilla
3 eggs, divided
1 T. butter
6 bananas, sliced
1 package vanilla wafer cookies

Mix 3/4 cup sugar, flour and milk together in a boiler on low heat, stirring until smooth. Add the beaten egg yolks, vanilla and butter. Continue to cook on low heat until it is thick, stirring occasionally. Pour the pudding over the layered bananas and wafers. For a topping, beat the egg whites until stiff. Beat in the remaining 1/4 cup sugar and pour over the pudding. Brown in the oven under the broiler.

Judy Mills
Lucedale, MS

Yum Yums

2 egg yolks
1/2 cup butter or lard
1-1/2 cups brown sugar, divided
1-1/2 cups flour, sifted 3 times
2 tsp. baking powder
1 tsp. vanilla
1 cup finely chopped walnuts
2 egg whites, beaten stiff

Mix together the egg yolks, butter, 1/2 cup brown sugar, flour, baking powder and vanilla. Press into the bottom of a 9 x 9 inch pan. Add a layer of walnuts, gently pressing into the bottom layer. Mix the egg whites and remaining 1 cup of brown sugar and spread over the top. Bake for 20 minutes at 350°.

Linda Knecht
Ames, IA

Cottage Cheese Cheesecake

1-1/4 cups graham
cracker crumbs
1 cup butter or margarine,
melted, divided
1 T. sugar
2 cups fat-free small
curd cottage cheese
2 8-oz. packages fat-free
cream cheese, softened
1 16-oz. carton fat-free
sour cream
1-1/2 cups sugar
4 eggs, beaten
3 T. all-purpose flour
3 T. cornstarch
1 T. plus 1 tsp. lemon juice
1 tsp. vanilla extract

Combine the crumbs, 1/2 cup butter and 1 T. sugar. Mix well and press into a 10-inch springform pan. Set aside. Blend the cottage cheese in an electric blender until smooth, turning the blender off every 15 seconds to scrape down the sides. Combine the cottage cheese and the remaining ingredients in a large mixing bowl and beat until fluffy Pour the mixture into the crust. Bake at 325° for 1 hour and 20 minutes. Turn off the oven and allow the cheesecake to remain in the oven for an additional 2 hours. Chill overnight.

Yields 10-12 servings.

Ursula Dybdahl
Pinebluff, NC

Bread Pudding with Warm Whiskey Sauce

Pudding:
4-6 slices bread, toasted
4 eggs
2 cups milk
1/2 cup sugar
1/2 tsp. cinnamon
1/2 tsp. vanilla
1/3 cup raisins

Sauce:
1/4 cup butter
1/2 cup sugar
1 egg yolk
2 T. water
2 T. whiskey

To make the pudding: Mix all of the ingredients together and place in a baking pan. Bake for 35-45 minutes in a 325° oven. To make the sauce: Melt the butter and add the sugar, egg yolk and water. Cook until clear or boiling. Remove from the heat and let it sit for 1 minute. Add the whiskey and serve over the warm pudding.

Tracy Callow
Stevensville, MD

Peach Pie

Crust:
2-1/2 cups flour
1 T. sugar
1/4 tsp. nutmeg
1 tsp. salt
2/3 cup vegetable oil
1/4 cup skim milk
Filling:
3/4 cup granulated sugar
1/4 cup flour
1/2 tsp. lemon peel
2 T. lemon juice
1/4 tsp. nutmeg
1 tsp. cinnamon
1/8 tsp. salt
4 cups peaches, peeled and sliced
1 T. margarine
Top crust:
reserved dough
2 T. flour
1 T. sugar

To make the crust: Mix the flour, sugar, nutmeg and salt together. With a fork, whip together the oil and milk. Pour the oil and milk mixture over the flour and blend with a fork until dampened. Reserve about 1/3 of the dough for top crust. Press the remaining dough evenly against the bottom and sides of a pie plate. Place in a 425° oven for 5 minutes and then remove. Allow to cool.

To make the filling: Combine all of the ingredients, except for the peaches and margarine. Place half of the sliced peaches in the pie dish and sprinkle with half of the sugar mixture. Repeat, then dot with margarine.

To the reserved dough add the flour and sugar. Mix until it resembles coarse peas. Sprinkle the dough over the pie and press down firmly to form a top crust. Bake in a 425° oven for 40-50 minutes, or until the crust is nicely browned.

Makes 8 servings.

Gaelen McNamara
Chattanooga, TN

Apple Pudding with Caramel Sauce

Pudding:
2 cups sugar
1/2 cup butter, softened
2 eggs, beaten
2 cups flour
2 tsp. baking soda
1 tsp. cinnamon
1 tsp. nutmeg
6 medium apples
1/2 cup chopped
walnuts (optional)
Caramel sauce:
1 cup butter
1 cup half-and-half
1 cup brown sugar
1 cup granulated sugar
1 tsp. vanilla extract

To make the pudding: In a large bowl, cream together the sugar and butter. Add the eggs. In a separate bowl, mix the flour, baking soda, cinnamon and nutmeg. Add to the creamed mixture. Peel, core and shred the apples in a food processor. Stir in the walnuts, if desired. Pour into a 9 x 13 inch pan and bake at 350° for approximately 35-40 minutes, until a toothpick stuck in the center comes out clean. Cool and cut into pieces.

To make the caramel sauce: Combine all of the sauce ingredients in a saucepan and cook over low heat for approximately 10 minutes.

Sandy McKenzie
Braham, MN

Index

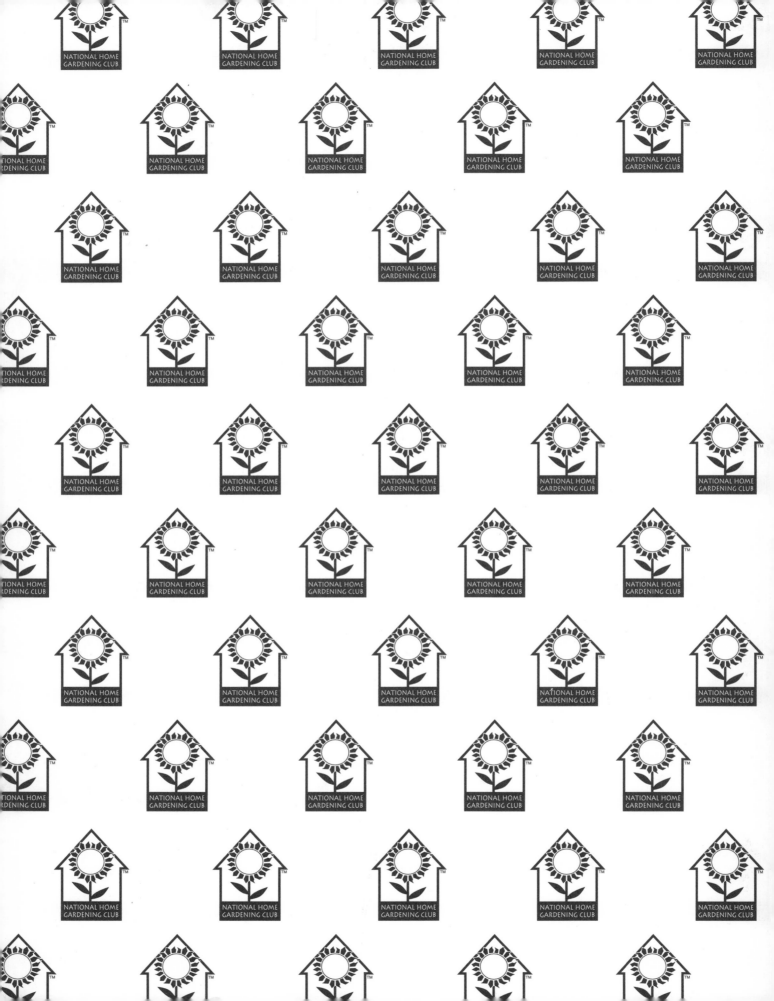